I0529817

Ridiculous and Ill-Advised

Rale Sidebottom

GLASSSPIDERPUBLISHING

Copyright ©2022 Rale Sidebottom

ISBN: 978-1-957917-22-1
Library of Congress Control Number: 2022922020

All rights reserved. No part of this book may be reproduced, stored in a retrieval system, or transmitted in any form or by any means without prior written permission from the author, except for the use of brief quotations in a book review.

This is a (mostly) true story.

Cover art by Theo Ellsworth
Published by Glass Spider Publishing
www.glassspiderpublishing.com

"We were outcasts, the people that
no one wanted to be, doing things
no one wanted to do, and nobody understood."

-Jeff Grosso

Prologue

THAT I WAS KIDNAPPED from the parking lot of a rock concert on New Year's Eve should tell you how far I had let my guard down.

Stolen away, against my will, disappeared into the night like a scene from a movie that depicts my partner in the events of the evening scratching his head in an empty parking lot at three in the morning in Oakland, California. Frantic calls to friends and family unanswered, cops on the case, everyone panicking. And then, three days later, when I call from a phone booth somewhere in New Mexico saying in fact I was *never* coming back, would that be the best starting point? Would you guess it was some sort of cult? An unmarked van, headed for nowhere and nothingness, weird, dark magician at the wheel, a head full of crazed ideas, monsters preying on the edge of all that is fun and dangerous, is this the best place to pull that cosmic trigger?

Because we're not doing that. That would be a disservice to fans of the almost lost art of vanishing into thin air if we jumped in right there, so we're going back just a bit further that same evening to a moment that seemed to crystallize and make clear everything that came after. Because there is such a thing as too little.

As with all good trips, set and setting is crucial. Downtown San Jose, December 31st, 1989, is the place we'll lay out the particulars of that night I left for good, forevermore, leaving the key that to this day sits on a ledge, abandoned and rusting in the elements, above a door that no longer closes properly.

Decades later, it's still there. That very room I once lived in, an overgrown garage abandoned to the rawest and most base of components, slowly fading into the earth, in a city that has settled into its foundations and has lost its sense of magic, a city that no longer participates in human dreams.

Fuck you, San Jose. It wasn't me—it was you.

SAN JOSE, 1989

1

RIDING A SKATEBOARD while coming on to an acid trip is not as nerve-racking as you might think. It can be extremely exciting, depending on your knowledge with or understanding of such a cavalier mixing of lifestyle cocktails. Push, push, push; tilt and lean into your reactions, reflexes quick and silent as a trained beast gliding into the night. Drag your foot, watch for cars, run the light. I'm always looking slightly ahead for stray pebbles that can throw me for a crash, keeping my eyes to the future but always looking all ways, listening for sounds that may affect the journey, reverberations. Balance is an afterthought. I've been riding my entire life but now, as I move into the evening, faster and faster, balance makes all the connections and circuits hum and jive at just the right amount. Tonight's addition is just another wave, another set.

Historically, skateboarding has always been the little cousin of the psychedelic, a sympathetic energy that rolls along, a simulation of other things, a drive to flow from one reality into the next. Both similarly synthesized, LSD as a search for respiratory and circulatory stimulation, and skateboarding as more of the same. The two were invented within ten years of each other and the more adventurous of the coming generations were quickly married in a union of necessity; new members of the "let's go faster" clique that follows no one and leads the march against normality in response to an era that's about to close.

Everything has a beat, a rhythm that catches the ear, and these days I'm starting to hear the soundtrack to the film that is eye. The sun sets through splayed ancient oaks, lanky limbs that throw strange shadows across my mind. I see everything cinematically. A quick beer run to the mini mart is devolving into a flash of glow mechanics.

My inability to sit still had me skateboarding by the age of ten, and now, a decade later, I'm zooming down San Carlos Street, on and off the sidewalk, into the street and back again, wind in my face, dodging poorly paved black holes and treacherous cracks in the sidewalks that could instantly toss me back to earth. The clickety clack manic heart attack of hard wheels across cracks, metronoming my ride, can you hear it? Into the store I go.

"You look like a ghost," says the girl behind the counter, avoiding my eyes.

"I wish" I reply, waiting for her to take my money, register proof of my existence. I look her in the eye. She knows it too.

"Goodnight, Dracula" she says, handing me my change.

"Well, which is it -ghost or vampire?", I respond as I exit the sliding glass door, six-pack in hand. She laughs as I disappear into the night.

Across asphalt and aggregate I move past your window and then gone again, far away/so close. Tonight's oncoming cacophony clicks into a rhythm that instantly bounces invented bass lines in my head, fuzz bass all distorted and dirty becoming something unique near song; that atonal tune that to the monsters in my mind I might describe as the sound of my soul when I know it's really just brought on by my jutting, jerky alertness to sudden movements, hidden faders and volume knobs twiddled and twisted by something in my brain that tracks along, ready for additions. Something close behind, chasing.

As I cruise past San Jose State, something deep in my skull creates theme music, scoring the quivering feeling in my gut, the tempo to my interior cinema getting weird. Shadows move and I flinch, laugh and try to shake it off, but I can't. The sounds of breathing chase me. I see altered reality coming to fruition, beaming dark ideas into my ride. I've probably taken too much, but no matter. Faster and faster, I glide through the abyss.

Neighborhood streets this time of night are always interesting. People returning home from a busy day, children lingering in the yards and parks, the late-nighters chatter over coffee at the market as they head into cemetery shifts at hospitals and security centers across the valley. On this last night of the decade, however, heading into the final of three thousand and one nights, a decade's worth of washed up and tossed out revelries and drudgeries, it's enough to strike in my core the feeling there's something circling—coming for me. It's almost dark and soon it will live.

The zzz zzz/click of my wheels suddenly downshift to a soft, muffled drone. I lose speed and without taking my feet off the board, I roll to a complete stop in soft dirt, paused, listening. The pavement has ended, I'm back on dirt alley. Quiet now, listening to the buzzing drone with the stillness of a beginning.

All alleys have the same genetic makeup. I've always been fascinated by the narrow stretches that line the back of every suburban block, existing for the purposes of off-street parking, keeping everything up front looking tidy and tight, offering somewhere to dump dirty mattresses and garbage. The secret, prying sections of choking invasives are allowed to thrive, multiply, and build micro-civilizations. Abandoned, rusted metals and tossed trash bags, evidence of poor living and unexceptional tenancy, all overgrown by years of meddling Himalayan blackberries which define the world beyond the backyard, music from the other side of the fence.

The narrowness of the unpaved lane keeps everything quiet and sheltered from the outside world, hiding the less appealing parts of our crummy constructs and fabricated futures. The hidden, the true. Ancient societies had alleys, we have them, their mission always discreetness. Skaters like myself are forever grateful to our allies the alleys that conceal us from inflamed authorities and irate neighbors as we flee through the night, running from the laws of this land when urethane wheels make poor transport.

We're skaters, living in poorly maintained garages and apartments across the city, paying as little as possible to live as high as we can. The shameless ways in which we occupy our days leave everything to chance and constant change and therefore blustering, braggardly stories loaded with adventure and action. We're full of shit and on fire, cheap rides packed with smart-ass boys and kick-ass girls, skateboards, worn-out knee pads and helmets that hold an unbelievable stink. Empty two liters of soda and forties of malt liquor litter the trunk and floorboards of our hundred-dollar cars.

We're the madness that invades the empty swimming pool in your yard when you leave town for the weekend, accessible by—you guessed it—the alley. Secret entrances and exits. Seasoned skaters can spot, in a second, any number of potential barriers, lines of sight for meddling neighbors who may or may not have a pool in their back yard for us to trash.

As opposed to skateboarding, all other sports have dedicated squads, teams and line ups that define themselves in clear relationship to a game, or a number. Their goal is to win. We joke that our stated goal is to lose, a reality of a different design. If you're a real participant in our culture and can abandon the false flag trifecta of goals, points, and playbooks and are hopelessly fixated on the sloped concrete walls and rickety but always gnarly rideable wooden halfpipes we construct in our parents' backyards, then you know - this was no joke. Our camaraderie is more brotherhood and family than teams organized into clearly defined goal-setting mode. We live and breathe skating in a way that more closely resembles drug addiction than sportsmanship. We don't play games.

In 1981, every state in America had at least one skatepark. Many had over twenty. Then, thanks to frivolous lawsuits and fear of financial ruin, one by one park owners simply closed shop, and by 1989 you could count the number left on one hand. America giveth, and America taketh away. As an endangered species, we're flagrant and obsessive in our hunts for new spots to hit, the best of us warriors on missions, fueled by Gatorade and dope, eager to take the drop and find a new pool to ride, if only for an afternoon. We lavish praise on one another when someone nails a good move, heckle them mercilessly if they bail, all of it a juvenile encouragement that reminds us we didn't fit in anywhere else. It doesn't help our standing with the general home-owning public that we spray-paint the walls of every pool we skate with obscure band names like Venom and Slayer.

I'm not great, but I've learned from the some of the best. The company I keep in the pursuit of mayhem schools me in a way not unlike a training camp, if the camp was skate marines or some radicalized band of hoodlums, out for some afternoon destruction to the normality and order of American idealism.

The ability to surveil a dozen different variables in our attempts to discreetly jump fences and keep our heads down so we could ride an empty swimming pool was something you learned quick, or you were out. Clandestine behavior was instrumental. Abandoned homes with pools half full of dark, disgusting sludge was no problem. Bucket brigades and a bunch of towels render any such scenario skatable in an hour. Immediacy drives our ethos. Our thoughts race while we try to make sense of situations before us: to jump the fence or not. Unaware of the lessons I was inherently learning, I became a scout. I was the eagle-eye that spotted variables before anyone else.

"Here comes a car!"

"Yeah, but look at the driver. She's seventy-five if she's a day. She'll never even hear us."

"See that neighbor on his porch over there? He sees us climb out of this car with skateboards and walk into the alley, he's on the phone in ten seconds. Keep driving."

Always sidestep conflict but keep your eye on the prize.

The exact mark—the end of an era and the beginning of another—is always hard to pinpoint, especially for an individual. For a generation, sure. An assassination here, a bombing or a virus there, the end of a series of increasingly tightened ropes will eventually break and give way to a cascade of new directions, for good or ill. History is full of kidnappings and ransoms paid, jailbreaks and corrosions of conformity that give way to the future.

For a person, the future is preceded by a series of events that slowly evolve into something else, for better or worse. The exact day? Many would argue there isn't such a thing. Time is a gradual, unstoppable force that along the way has a hundred indicators, warning signs, messages and dreams that would at the very least hint at what, logically, would come next. Science dictates such things. But I'm pretty sure, if my notes are correct, that in my life it began the night we took Garfield the Cat LSD.

Alleys remind me of how I want to make movies but instead I'm taking acid; taking the back roads instead of getting with the program and hitting the pavement that makes that trip to the future smoother, less bumpy. I survey my surroundings that have now begun to shimmer with that tip over the psychedelic edge, the subconscious excitement of stranger things to expand in my subcontinent, that feeling when one is acutely aware of the chemical imbalances running through their system. I see all as art, my life the opening sequence of a slasher film, a neo-noir. The angles, the tracking shots, the harrowing notes of doom from the garage beyond.

Just a few blocks south of here, abandoned shopping carts are piled high, a massive, empty lot with thousands upon thousands, waiting for reclamation or destruction, harbingers of doom that echo in my mind as I pass them every morning, reminding me of our endless trash problem. How many of those piles exist in the world? What will happen to them? To us? How will we get rid of all this shit? Blinking crosswalk lights click-click-click in the distance, the periphery of my vision a flashing caution.

My hearing is amplified by psychedelic synesthesia. I catch snippets of conversation from the other side of the fence. People laughing up the alley behind the market, sports radio in a garage somewhere (you can tell what kind of room by the imbalance of sound—cavernous and poorly insulated), discussing how the Forty-Niners have punished every team they've played this year, by an average of twenty-one points a game, a fact that is punctuated by heavy sighs from an upstairs window. Must be a Raiders fan.

"Post-season is here, Montana and the boys are ready for the contenders..."

A smattering of emotions creep into my consciousness from every angle: despair, excitement, anguish, and compassion. These are all signals in my void, a message from others living their lives. I find myself jealous but mostly curious as to the origins of their existence. Forgeries of reality catch and lie to my eyes. The lie in the middle of believe.

I click my skateboard into hand and stride into the overgrown yard where my converted garage lies, the man inside awaiting my return. Stepping in, I stop and stare at the breathing wood paneling, in and out, my cheap, dumpster-dived carpet now iridescent waves; sets of life breathing in, breathing out, *hawoo hawooosshh, howaa howaaassh*, a rush into my head with the cosmic confluence of time attempting to freeze in amber and keep all these memories alive for my amusement as I age and fade, far, far away; into the future.

I smile, close my eyes and, for just a moment, the shudder of the universe comes into me, through me. Faster now. I am Galactica. I am mud baths and statuary, glistening golden elephant deities, collapsing by the thousands into the future, a cascading renegading waterfall of observance and then -blink and breathe deep-, in through the nose, out through the mouth and back again. A phone ringing in the distance dings me back to normal time and space, my overgrown backyard on south 16th Street.

"I am the son," I say to the universe as I cross the room.

I crack a beer and take a sip. Thinking I might have something, I toss a cold one to the space cadet in sunglasses and cutoffs splayed out on my couch, sit down at my typewriter, and check to see if anything useful spews itself out of the ether that might help me pass my screenwriting class.

EXT. OAKLAND COLISEUM PARKING LOT - NIGHT

TEXT O/S - December 31, 1989

Thousands of people mill about, all in attendance for the
Grateful Dead's annual NEW YEARS EVE concert. Near the center
of this mass of party goers, row upon row of wildly painted,
double decker SCHOOL BUSES form a virtual city within a city.

This is SHAKEDOWN STREET, the psychedelic marketplace for all
things weird and illegal. From T-shirt and burrito vendors to
LSD and dope dealers, it's all here.

Shitty audio recordings from the band's previous concerts
blare from the giant buses and a medley of VW vans, station
wagons, and ragged vehicles plastered with bumper stickers
representing every movement, cause and concern known to man.

Passing into the crowd, we see license plates from many
states. The event is widely known in underground circles. The
tightly parked buses form long avenues resembling a joyful
apocalypse of dropout culture, handmade and virtually
invisible to the outside world.

INT. OLD STATION WAGON - SAME

In the back seat, window down, JOAN and FRANK, both 23 and
adorable in floppy homemade hats and tie dye skirts, pass a
joint back and forth, smiling at passerby. In the way back
sits their big black lab BOOM BOOM.

GLENDA THE GOOD WITCH, 21, cute with wild red hair on her way
somewhere, stops and leans in.

                    GLENDA
          Hey, can I get a hit?

Smiles from Frank and Joan. Frank hands it to her.

                    FRANK
               Take it, pass it on. Brought in a
               bunch from Oregon. Happy New Year!

Glenda smiles, leans in and gives him a kiss on the cheek.
Joan smiles back.

                    GLENDA
               All right! Right on, brother. Well,
               off to see the Wizard!

WATCHING THROUGH THE REAR VIEW MIRROR we see her walk away, dragging an old broom behind her. Wizard of Oz meets Oakland parking lot. Joan and Frank make out.

EXT. PARKING LOT - SAME

Camera tracks through the crowd. Sweater-wearing college professors feeling their radical roots and first year kids attending Berkeley, deadhead grad students on the road from all points east. Small town farm boys and girls from the central valley and down Gilroy and Salinas way, the lot is a medley of true American roots.

From hippies and punks to Goth kids and proto-Burning Man types, in from the suburbs to buy drugs and cruise the weird America scene to high school jocks looking for mushrooms, everyone is here.

Pulsing near the center of the transportable city is the DRUM CIRCLE. Twenty-odd shirtless male drummers (women too; this is Goddess territory) on every form of Congo, bongo and percussive instrument you can think of are, in spite of all the anarchy around them, remarkably organized. The beat is steady and throbbing, all around them a swirl of sexy men and witchy women dance and spin to the magic of the last night of the nineteen eighties.

Several TORCHES and dozens of burning incense bundles transform the scene to ancient ritual.

One muscular drummer in the center, WIZARD, 40-ish in massive dreadlocks, clouds of swirling incense and sage smoke almost obscuring him, cries out to all.

                    WIZARD
          Let the darkness part, and let love
          shine on this new decade!

The crows roars its approval. Everyone is HIGH AS FUCK. Literally, figuratively and in all ways primordial and cosmic, this crowd is on fire. The drumming grows faster and louder, vendors nearby even stand to witness the peak, the explosive end of the jam coming right up.

Some pranksters decides now is the right time to light off a couple dozen bottle rockets. They're right.

From beyond the dancing crowd, creeping up into the lot from the dark bay of Oakland and moving towards them is THE MONSTER, age unknown.

PARKING LOT - SAME

Thirty feet tall, he roars across the freeway, cars skidding
in every direction. His blood soaked, scaly skin and
freakish, mutant heads, eyes like burnt blistered onions and
mouths full of teeth sharp as razors glimmer in the street
lights in anticipation of the destruction he's about to
wreak.

As he leaps across the 680 and slams into the parking lot of
the concert, multiple demonic heads rear back and thrill in
the fear of the crowd.

The police, seeing this thing, have no alternative: kill or
be killed.

Concert goers scream and flee as the cops FIRE at the monster
- he's just an it to them - and he shreds and tears asunder
all in his path, making his way across the lot, captured by
bloodlust, oily scales and hairy arms flowing a dark blue and
purple incandescence, looking like some monstrous wolf but
also akin to something from beyond the stars.

He moves to the drum circle, a group completely unaware of
the madness and death coming towards them just beyond the row
of buses and vans. He swats at cops, hippies, and others
unlucky enough to be caught in his path.

Limbs fly, blood splays. Bullets don't faze him.

He rises up to full height above the buses and, throwing back
his heads, emits a primordial roar. It is the last thing many
will ever hear.

INT. OLD STATION WAGON- SAME

Frank sees the monster but laughs, thinking it's just his
imagination.

                    FRANK
                 (smiling)
             Cool...

DRUM CIRCLE - SECONDS LATER

Exploding fireworks punctuate the rousing finale as the
drummers rise in noise and energy. The dancers howl and spin
wildly.

Wizard drops a gigantic BOOM on his massive conga as the colorful explosions light the crowd and then wham – all drummers stop. The beast dissipates into a giant 'poof' of smoke and dust.

The silence lasts for a second more before the crowd erupts in a roar of cheers, clapping and smiles, laughter and hugs, a lighting of joints, all passed around, until stranger upon stranger has smoked them down to the roach.

Typing while on LSD is not an ideal activity. The clacking and clicking of manual keys starts to sound like bugs, insects trying to riot in my walls, so I knock it off. Time to focus on the situation at hand. Current circumstances dictate that I focus on this guy in cut offs on my couch who has asked to be referred to as 'Jeff the Elder'.

2

I WAS ELEVEN going in, twenty-one coming out. 80s punk, not just as a sound but as a way of life, got into my system early. Pre-diagnosis ADHD kids with wild ideas and plans to subvert everything, waiting out the doldrums of pop culture by smoking pot in the back parking lot of Thrifty's Drugs. Drinking beer in the suburbs that surrounded our schools, building half pipes and skating into the night, all of it a grand adventure if you knew where and how to look. The acid came a little later but seemed to come right on time. Not too young, get it done with by the time we finish college. Maybe.

Leaning back, I take a breath and stare at my hands, now rising and sinking like monster flesh, shimmering against blood and bone, shake my head, remember I'm flunking out of college—a new low for me. I've never been the motivated kind and I'm spending a lot of time doing next to nothing and contemplating what I *don't* want to do with my life.

With the right attitude, it's not very challenging to figure out how to isolate yourself from expectations. Living in a poorly converted garage behind a friend's parent's house, I'm two years into my junior college illusions, all faked pragmatism in that I'm trying to convince others that I'm genuinely interested in being here, half-listening to boring lectures on a campus full of what will become the Internet's first domain squatters and third level programmers. The smart people are over at Stanford and Berkeley.

I'm living on stolen land, and everything is starting to shimmer in that way that only a good batch of acid can bring. The chemist that makes his mark with his own brand of psychedelic is often felt in the first thirty minutes or so. You get the feeling he's trying to change the world, or he's just got an axe to grind against the chemistry professor who flunked him can seem to come through your pores and tell you if things are going well or not. Look around, take a breath.

Sooner or later life's gonna creep up and grab me and put me somewhere if I don't do something, probably one of those dead-end hope machines of some falsely fabricated sort, the kind of place people go "oh cool, you work there?" but it makes you gag, the employer that makes you tuck in your shirt and stop wearing shorts everywhere but as much as I inherently know this, I'm ignoring it.

I'm enrolled at West Valley Junior College, and in addition to my screenwriting class, I'm taking art theory, prepping for a life of lo-fi art projects and abstract scrap metal installations that bear more resemblance to trash piles than thought-provoking commentaries on the social contract. I know this because my first piece was in a show that promised just such commentary but was panned by the school paper as "kids with too much time and dope on their hands."

While I'm ambivalent about my current options that are, to be fair, totally of my own doing, I'm not a complete loser. I'm also in a noise band, which, in 1989, is a blast and not only part of a larger scene up and down the West Coast, but also worthy of getting booked pretty consistently around the Bay Area.

I work part-time downtown at the Comic Collector shop, catching up on generations of underground narratives and absorbing knowledge of obscure artists like Moebius, Lynda Barry and Vaughn Bodé, spending the rest of my time hanging out with a loose-knit assemblage of local ne'er-do-wells, doing drugs and banging on metal.

Improvisational music and working with experimental composers can prepare you for life in ways that are unknown to the people unfamiliar with Miles Davis, John Cage, Thelonious Monk and the new guard, guys like John Zorn and Caspar Brotzmann, Merzbow and Melt-Banana. There's something deeper in music than anything else, purer than the images and light we've always taken as truth. Sound affects and moves through us into new ways of responding to others, asking questions that don't have answers. Listening more than playing can help forge our own set of ethics and responsibilities, and I discover that the power to change the energy of a room with others is only possible when I listen.

The band I'm in is weird, and while the project's true nature was initially lost on me, the radical and avant-garde ideas will later become gristle, feeding the meat on my brain for years to come. I'm heavily influenced by my music classes with Lou Harrison, an old-school member of the American Avant-Garde, but in the beginning, I was just trying to be cool and meet girls. It was Lou's classes that formed my lifelong love for modern and experimental composition. I love all the weirdo noise bands we meet at shows and parties, but I've never found being an audience member at gatherings like those particularly satisfying. Just listening to people squealing away on power tools or destroying robot toys while forcing feedback out of guitar amps is only fun if I'm doing it.

Still, I'm a kid from Morgan Hill, a bit of a hick in matters of taste, music, and culture; a high school dropout, a know-nothing from the sticks, kicking around the embers of one scene as the next is about to explode. I'm keen for influences, and it was music and the freedom of chance that started my journey.

In the interest of "true" art, our band has only three rules:
1) no songs.
2) no practice.
And most importantly:
3) no funny.

This last rule is crucial, because if you're a crazy, out of control, avant-garde noise outfit and you don't take yourselves seriously, no one else will either. It works, barely. At any given show, an indiscriminate number of "musicians" show up at the venue, bearing instruments (in my case it was simply cast-off scrap metal, used as percussion with soft mallets that occasionally sounds otherworldly, but mostly just obnoxious and harsh).

We all take the oath: no songs, no jams or drum circle style get-togethers. Serious and heavy, the no-funny rule was imposed more as the artist component, to keep a couple of us in line who are always likely to fall into some horrible stand-up comedy during our sets. No time for laughter— this stuff is serious. Can the editor of the feminist 'zine *Hangy Thing* rant diatribes on stage as we blare our particular brand of freak out? Absolutely. Can the strange guitar kid we found living down by the tracks join in? Please do. Butoh practitioners? You're in. Wannabe post-everything spoken word poets? All are welcome. We get the occasional gig at the Cactus Club or Marsugi's downtown, opening for unheard-of groups like Nirvana and Vomit Launch.

The fact that we're even getting booked at these places with these kinds of bands is an indicator that San Jose is up for grabs. Anything is possible, everything was happening, and no one worries about what tomorrow might bring. The Bay Area is in *a moment*; a time when a great thaw revealed the city around us in ways that only became clear many years later. As in all things, it's pretty much a template. There's a common thread between all so-called 'cool' places in America. Before the culture capitalists and harbingers of death and decay arrive in their pressed slacks of doom and snide eyes that jack rents and destroy flavor, passion and true electricity of the soul. For us, it has to be dangerous and cheap, an air of crime and insanity helps; the more dangerous, the better.

First, they pitch it as cool. Then, it's marketed and sold as cheap and affordable. Then, somehow, it quickly becomes neither. Technology coming into the common consciousness of the Bay Area was decades in the making. The city is awakening and the best we can say about this time is that we are present; we skate, and we have a band. Everyone hates our music, and we hate them back. It's a total blast. My mind has already begun to be rewired. I'm just leaning away instead of leaning in because I feel like an outsider; everyone seems much cooler than me and I linger on the edges, nervous to take my place in the great drama unfolding here.

I don't know when, or even if, I ever knew that I would make monster movies, I couldn't come up with any articulated way of saying it back then. I guess it's just a hunch, some idea that lingers in the back of your mind, like a beast under cover of night. Most evenings we would sit in Ajax or the Cactus Club, shooting quarter games of pool, some cheap drinks, and generally waiting to see what'll happen. Then, Mark the Narc comes in and says, "Hey, the Ledge is playing a basement over on 18th street," and leaves.

I don't know who the Ledge is, but others do, and a show is a show, and we understand —we need to go.

An hour later, we're sitting on a porch drinking beers and waiting around for the Ledge to appear, chatting up the residents as people from all over drift in. Old music cats with long hair and dirty glasses and fresh-pressed young girls all file into the basement to await his arrival. Ken Woods, our DJ buddy from KSJS and once coworker at Wherehouse Records wanders in with a little cassette recorder, ready to document anything, everything.

A homeless looking guy with a shopping cart covered in blankets wanders along. He stops in front of us, bursts out with a dramatic "Look what I found," whipping off the blankets to reveal hundreds of old 45s. My buddy Mike and I take a look, and they are indeed good picks. From C.W. McCall to Herman's Hermits to Billy Eckstine and cheap-o kid's discs, it's a real good pile.

"Someone's throwing them away, I said no way and chance put me there as they hit the street, so I grabbed this cart lickety split and here we are!" His smile is contagious, and I ask who he is.

"Why, I'm the Legendary Stardust Cowboy," he says, "is this where I'm supposed to play?" He parks the cart out back and pulls his gear out from the bottom rack, hidden by records, a single guitar and a folded leather pouch of some kind.

"Can you point the way there, buddy?"

We escort the Ledge into the basement where he proceeds to unfold his leathers, a stunning set of beautifully colored, wild old cowboy chaps. He takes a few minutes to tune up his guitar, looking awesome now in old cowboy shirt and those chaps, flashing and twinkling in a dirty basement scene. Suddenly the lights go out. With only a string of old Christmas lights illuminating the room, he and his backup band (just a kid on drums and some old jazz bass player) rips into a set so amazing, so crazy and wild, it is confirmed to us yet again: San Jose is the place to be. Hot spot on the continent, none can dispute this. Everyone sways to the convulsing chords, the chaotic riff, the voice from another plane.

I look up and see a face peering in the basement window, realizing that out on the street, this guy I'm looking up at is on his hands and knees, looking in, seeing what he's missing. He scans the room, and when we make eye contact, I gesture to him to come on down, but then I see it in his face. He's freaked out. This guy is genuinely disturbed by the Ledge's signature song "Paralyzed," and there's no way we'll get him to venture underground with us. I laugh and turn away. The power of that night, and so many others, spurred me into belief. Belief that we were right, we were on the correct side of destiny, it was all ringing in my head, the whole thing of it all. Down here in the dirt, we're the real monsters of rock.

But back to Jeff the Elder. I'm standing in my converted garage apartment, surrounded by an overgrown yard littered with beer cans, looking out on the last sunset of the 80s, half watching the TV in the corner casting minor key string clusters from a perfect musical score to John Carpenter's (heavily edited for tv) *The Thing*.

Everything vibrates slightly; more than the typical New Year's buzz of energy, this shimmery fuzz of light and shadow coming off the subconscious of an entire generation about to leave behind this most abysmal of eras, this deathly decadent, hipster technicolor preppie death nightmare, was reason enough for us to drop some acid for dinner. It's clean—no strychnine tonight. Jeff speaks up.

"Man, I don't feel so good. I feel…bent."

Yeah, no kidding, I think. Nobody let this guy near a mirror for at least six hours.

We're jacked up on some Garfield the Cat tabs from a girl over in Willow Glen, little orange squares with a tiny, perfect Garfield stamped on each. So small, so strong. I sink into deep thought about my feet, thinking about skin, hair, and nails. I don't share my thoughts, as my partner in psychedelics this evening, Mr. Jeffery Demarco of the Bascomb Avenue Demarcos, wide-eyed and sprawled on my battered couch of inequity, is already having a hard time on the cat planet. While I'm starting to feel pretty groovy, he looks a little tight.

Tonight, I'm his babysitter while everyone else in the gang strong enough to handle heavy duty acid has already bailed for the Pink Floyd laser light show at the fairgrounds. They promise they're not leaving me totally in the lurch, just for a couple hours. Jen leans out the car window as they pull away, tossing her empty beer can into the neighbor's yard.

"Thanks for hanging with him. We'll be back before midnight."

It's fine with me, I don't care much for Pink Floyd *or* lasers.

When it comes to amateurs who've taken too much, I'm the guy they turn to, not afraid and more relaxed. I like monsters. Big fan. My ability to laugh off the heavy, inward hang ups that others fixate on when the synapses start to turn on themselves probably keeps the freak out cases close to my side. I'm stuck with Jeff tonight, but it's cool. He needs somebody to lean on, and if this feeling that I have flowing through my veins is any indicator, it's gonna be weird. We're on the edge of a black hole, and the pull is tangible.

Nights in the late 1980s for our generation were dedicated to one of three things: skateboarding, dollar movies at the UA theater, or staying home to watch TV. These spare options were all united by one thread— walking or skateboarding everywhere. Drinking, smoking weed, and doing drugs came with the territory. Given Jeff's state, *The Thing* probably wasn't the best film to put him in front of. It also didn't help his psyche to be in a poorly soundproofed garage while my backyard neighbor worked on his experimental industrial music. The glitches and clicks of analog drum machines crossed with out-of-tune keyboards constantly drifting in and out of earshot freaked Jeff out. Those sounds were more likely than anything to push him over the edge. Techno guy was ahead of his time, but that's downtown in 1989: misfit musicians, punks, skaters, tech nerds too early to be cool, underground comic artists and game writers who, unbeknownst to many of them, were about to become the things they so earnestly professed to hate—capitalists and titans of industry.

It is far from exaggeration to say that anyone who grew up in the Bay Area at that time can also name a handful of people who went from being boring, talentless hacks to millionaires in less than a decade simply because they were able to manipulate and cleanse their histories into something seemingly exotic, take a computer class or two, advance by light years and fail upwards into Silicon Valley's towers of prestige and power. In my experience, it was always the boring people. Those dreary, tiresome people who are all "yes sir" and always willing to kiss ass to make money. Don't take chances, don't stir the pot. It's actually the opposite of ideas, and a lot like Hollywood in that way, the Bay Area of the early 90s: be charismatic, bring a little money to the game, learn how to manipulate people and kiss ass and you're in.

I want something different, fantastically and madly different, something that doesn't require paperwork or degrees or letters of recommendation. I want to do things and be someone who wasn't spoken of proudly by his family. Not to embarrass them necessarily, I'm just yearning to flee, ready to take whatever steps necessary to find my own way, a way that doesn't cater to anything but rather subverts the very idea of way.

Something was born in me long ago; maybe I learned of it in a book or saw something, an image that escaped into me from a movie or a television show and set up camp, unwilling to leave, a virus, something as simple as an ingredients list from all the packaging I used to read as a kid. A private magic spell that was always unfolding, unwittingly following along, catching glimpses, never knowing that the great magical mystery of me was always being cast, getting ready for flight. Something in me yearned to break away, something crazed and eager to attain escape velocity.

It was at this age that I was starting to comprehend the power of cinema and the effect it was having over me. My inner workings, my ability to daydream scenarios and play out myths and fantasies in the real world concurrently. I was learning that the answers for me, while cinematic and dramatic, they were real, something alive. A narrative living somewhere outside the glaring suburban systems of understanding and accepted storylines that define the glut of the human race. I wanted wild breakouts and frantic chase scenes, monsters and maidens, wild trips into the great unknown. I wanted out, and I wanted in.

3

THE WAY IN is strange. I'd never known a way yet but receiving copies of both Kerouac's *Dharma Bums* and Robert Anton Wilson's *Cosmic Trigger* from my aunt when I was a kid kicked my ass. I was immediately caught in their tendril texts and synaptic snares. Throw in pulp romance novels, Sci-fi and the dozen or so magazines I always devoured, and I found I'd set the bar pretty high. As we trolled neighborhoods scouting for pools or skate spots, I was in the back seat reading comics or doing dramatic readings of the "real letters" section from Hustler's Forum to my cohorts, enjoying the camaraderie of adventure and mayhem that we encountered as we swept the Bay Area, from backyard ramps in San Francisco to old, abandoned pools out in Morgan Hill.

We're always on the search, usually for illegal turf, punishable by law, cops in pursuit, a kind of guttural magic that guided us straight into the chaos and general anarchy that goes with illegal behaviors, actions that can drive your heart mad, beating way too fast but hell, man! To jump fences through three backyards in the middle of the day with boards in hand to escape security guards who thought they would catch us and then what? Write us a ticket? Mere mortals. In the grand scope of things, we know they're the criminals, not us. Our afternoons often play out like a mystery novel or drug-addled search and rescue mission. And when at last we make a clean getaway, laughing, that's an adrenaline high that flushes itself through the tips of our fingers and makes the universe, finally, seem real.

From there I devoured fantasy and horror; books filled my backpack as I hit the road solo for the first time in the spring of 1988. Being young and impressionable, I was eager for experience, and had hitch-hiked around the West Coast a bit to get a feel for the flavor of it. Finding characters at every turn once I stepped off the grid, I was energized by the fact that I'd made allies of people who, like myself, were listening for the secrets and searching for the sounds. I was strapped for cash, but no matter: America is flush with opportunity, depending on your ethics, luck, and pluck. Hitchhiking is a lifestyle; finding inexpensive food and cheap (or free) lodging becomes second nature.

All of this was based primarily on meeting people, so I was constantly going through great social adventures as well. I slept in the ditches I skated, and even jumped the ocean to backpack across western Europe for several weeks, finding old, abandoned skate parks and following weird punk bands and noise artists, finding an energy in the road that was to become an underlying theme in my love of the unknown. That stuff hidden around the corner, where no one's looking. Spread out on my old sleeping bag, falling asleep in an apple orchard reading Clive Barker by flashlight, only to be awakened by the buzzing, killing attack of crop dusters, intent on dousing the world with chemicals and death. Growing up in orchard country, you're exposed to some pretty weird dirt.

By our late teens, everyone had already become hip, too cool because they've seen it all, know it all, too cool for school, too punk for the scene, too tough for everything. I was searching for a hidden world. Underground shows, pirate radio stations and wild-haired people, full of energy and passion. That was my America. I dreamt and fantasized a lot. It doesn't hurt to be underemployed and less than enthusiastic about things like jobs and rental agreements to help fuel the fire.

You had to have a gig though; there had to be a way to stay forever floating in the slipstreams of what we'd started to see as the new weird America. Rejecting the dominant culture just felt like the correct response to what I was feeling, but there was a secret missing, a page that had been ripped out. The cost of rejection, of course, a complete lack of empathy from family and friends. But the freedom, the opportunity to do it all on your own terms? To get as far out as you could and not fret the endless coming Mondays? That was worth more than a dozen collar shirts and a pile of paychecks with half taken out for military spending, any day.

Since the early 80s, touring punk bands with no money themselves had been slashing new paths into the hinterlands of the nation. Places where the freaks meet. Independent 'zines were made of the small enclaves of punks, weirdos, artists and minor league cultists hanging out in the small towns, the mid-sized enclaves too with small colleges and smaller venues. They had been photocopied and distributed for all, mostly at punk shows.

Being born in '68, I was a little behind those guys, but I was excited to find what I knew was, to my search, incredibly important information. Maps to the interior. I found my first copy of Maximum Rock n Roll at a Flipper concert in 1988, and it opened my mind to the possibilities of getting weird and staying there, forever. It illustrated all of it: the towns, how to book tours, where cheap hotels were, a 'musicians wanted' section.

The texts of American dropout culture are all there, from the vagabonding mendicants of the early 18th-century to latecomers like Burroughs and Bowles and Black Flag; I just had to put down the books, get it together and make my move. To grab it and keep it and never go back. The work ethic my father had instilled in me was there, I never wanted to be unemployed or living on someone else's dime whether it was the government's or anyone else's. I always tried to pay for my own ride. But working hard at something meaningless seemed, more and more, to be the whole American narrative, and that something sickened me and made me want to never stop vomiting. Plus, none of my friends were willing to take the leap. In all my thoughts and dreams, I felt alone.

As far back as I can remember, I've loved monsters. Monster movies from all eras, from silent films to today. I still love the jump scare, and misdirection in cinema is not dissimilar from a good LSD trip. I learned about the machinery of monster movie magic when I was ten.

Our babysitter broke down horror films for my sister and I like this: right where you can't see, just off the edge of this screen here, he told us, there's a bunch of people eating donuts and sipping coffee quietly, watching their creations live, standing just where you can't see them.

Craftsmen. Makeup people. Hairdressers. Working artists. Blood pumps. Torso builders and destroyers. Eyeball shredders. When you're a kid, learning there's a small crowd of people standing just out of shot on every film really opens your mind. Then, insane genius that our babysitter was, he pulls a magic trick, turning off the sound on the film Halloween and letting us watch the scarier scenes silent. That blew my ten-year old scalp off. Most scenes become lethargic and drag. Chase scenes become tedious, jump scares are nonexistent, and blood and guts moments are simply exercise and efforts in the futility of science and logic. Sound rules all movies, but none more than horror. The magic remained; the blood, the guts, the pure terror of it all was distilled and worked out into a seamless cinematic exercise constantly repeating in my mind; the best monster movies from the dawn of film to today live and die by the same three rules: Fear of the unknown, fear of family, and fear of rejection or failure.

There was a small but dedicated group of renegade filmmakers a couple years ahead of me in high school, and I tagged along with them every chance I got. The Caplener brothers and their assorted cast of wacko actors and wild musician friends inspired me to reassess my own ridiculous stories, let a little madness into the idea and distill it for a bit, then shoot. Video cameras were cheap and easy to run. I followed along as they shot endless videos of spy chases, murder mysteries, music videos and assorted ephemera, all under the guise of high school shenanigans, antihero capers with ludicrous story arcs. We were playing at life, discovering its true value by dissecting our favorite films and reverse engineering them in the most abstract and laborious ways possible. As we were figuring out how to make movies, we were learning how to make life.

The real monsters, the big bad boring ones, the ones that finished college, wore suits, got their heads screwed on tight and straight and went to a job every day, those ones bore the hell out of me. Or, as Steve Martin put it, "let's get all excited and go to a yawning festival." That shit scares me like nothing else. Many would agree—that's why that line in *On the Road* has been underlined so many times, you know the one: "*the only people for me are the mad ones, the ones who are mad to live, mad to talk, mad to be saved, desirous of everything, blah blah blah…"*

To this day I am always underwhelmed in those moments when I am forced to interact with real world monsters, ones who claim to love adventure but never really go—they just love the idea; whether coworkers, classmates, girlfriends or the sucker in the company break room (feet off the table, please) who thinks he going to make it big because he's reading the newest "how to join the top one percent of America" book. You don't even need to roll the dice in that game. Just go directly from school to school and job to job, to bed to bed to bed to bed.

Pay the bills, eat the pills, work towards that big two weeks of vacation, spend it in a cheap resort being catered to by the locals who hate you for the vermin you are. Retire and start to live life after your body's too tired to do anything and has lost the will to dance all night. I tell myself I'm on my way out of the system, that I will never play their games.

My screenwriting class at West Valley has gone poorly, and it's solely for my lack of effort. The writing I've actually done is alright, but I still skip my other classes to go skateboarding, another habit held over from high school, and I find myself teetering at the precipice of my educational career. I'm babysitting a guy on acid who will go on to become the owner of several KFC franchises, pondering my future, watching *The Thing*, my hairy toes shifting and shuddering in the dusk of night, when good old Jim, my drug buddy and dope dealer supreme, walks in.

"Check it out, lame boys."

He drops two tickets for tonight's Grateful Dead concert on a stack of TV guide's I'm stealing ideas from. Remember how I said I love the fear? Did you *read* the screenplay I just showed you? I think I just wrote the story of our evening in advance. Which is, of course, impossible. I go to the typewriter and look at the pages, my shaking hand picks them up, tension arising in my chest. I hadn't seen nor heard from Jim in weeks, had I? I can't recall. My stomach starts to churn. I need another beer.

"Okay, this is crazy, man. I mean, it's unsure, or rather, It's unlikely that…"

I can't even speak, not a good sign, so I just let him read the script. He glances up at me several times. After he finishes, he puts the pages aside and sits me down like a little kid.

"Don't be scared. It's on paper, man. You literally wrote it down. We gotta get to that show!"

I'm running my hands through my hair, unfocused gaze into the distance as he lights a smoke. He knows he's got me on the ropes.

"Plus, gonna need you to drive. I picked up another speeding ticket last week. No more license for six months." Nineteen years old. What a guy.

"I can't drive! I'm up shit creek as it is with my grades and my college career. Plus, I'm on acid."

"Career," he laughs, unnerved by the LSD. "What would you even do with a stupid theater degree? Move to Ashland?"

"I have to keep an eye on old Jefé here." We both look at Jeff and smile warily. He's scratching his nuts, eyes closed, listening to Kurt Russell curse the men around him through a howling wind.

Each time I protest, he ups the ante.

"I'll cover gas."

I tell him no way.

"I'll buy beers. Let's do this! The gate is opening!" He's persistent. I've now got a free concert ticket and beers when I get there, plus, the advantage of a pre-scripted evening. What could go wrong?

"Dude, the forecast was written by you, man! It's crazy if we don't go now. Monsters killing hippies, it's like the greatest movie never made!" He laughs, and I have to stop thinking too much, can't lose it now, it's too early on New Year's Eve. Way too early to skip out. I look at Jeff, seemingly asleep on the couch.

"Is he okay?" Jim asks.

Eyes closed, Jeff pipes up.

"I'm fine, idiots. I just peaked a little bit ago. You can bail; I'm fine. Just chain me to this couch before the moon rises." I still try and get out of this.

"I can't take the chance. If I get busted, I'm…no way. I'd love to but I can't."

Jim won't leave. He just smokes a couple cigarettes in the yard, then laughs when I cave.

"Great. Hurry up. I'll be in the van." He tosses me the keys. In slow motion they spiral and spin through the air, a kaleidoscopic trail spinning behind them and I think, *I'm driving?* Whatever.

When you're properly psychedelicized and it's clean and right, the cosmos can light up and tell you the safety word for future. I buzz on the sense of the coming evening, while still in total darkness about the fact that I may not be back for a minute.

This is one of LSD's great mysteries; it can't be explained, really, but anyone who has taken enough and has leaned into the positive possibility curve in the depths of the primordial ooze that is our brains will agree: we're going for a big ride tonight on the Karma cosmic highway, so better make sure you're ready. I lean over and kiss Jeff on the forehead, wish him a Happy New Year. I stink my head under the hose (my sink), throw on a clean sweatshirt and grab my skateboard. A wad of cash (forty-two bucks), stuff my wallet into my back pocket.

About to walk out, I stop and look back at Jeff one more time. His eyes are open now, and we have that weird moment where, for just an instant, everything is charged with meaning and powerful, deep as a river of cosmic sludge flowing out of and through both of us. Neither of us could possibly realize that we'll never see each other again, but we hold the moment, unsure of the universes' forces that are reaching through us, and I go to my little bookshelf and grab *Pull Your Own Strings* by Wayne Dyer, a self-help guy who I don't find totally ridiculous and actually kind of awesome. In the book, Dyer criticizes the 'hurry up' culture so blatantly on display in 1980s America. I hand it to Jeff.

"Here, this'll bring you down." I switch the TV channel so he can catch the opening of Captain Cosmic and his New Year's Eve broadcast of *Godzilla vs. Megalon*. He smiles as he puts on his sunglasses and tucks the book into the front of his pants and gives me a smile, Dr. Wayne Dyer's face poking out over his zipper.

"Later, dude."

Two hours later, Jim and I are playing drums, even higher now on beer and mushrooms, enjoying the Grateful Dead's parking lot scene at the Oakland Coliseum, a real demolition derby of all things 80s.

I'm trying my best not to think about the monster that, according to my writing, should be popping up any minute to annihilate everyone. Dogs, drugs and drummers everywhere. Lowballing, denim-clad acid dealers, shirt pockets literally overflowing with sheets of LSD.

"Doses for sale! Three for five!" he screams to the masses. A wide swath of humanity's greatest shitheads, all congregating for the death of the 80s party. 1990 is three hours away.

4

THE TICKETS WERE fake.

Jim didn't know, of course. He got them from a guy at Streetlight Records and now, after waiting in line all the way up the winding asphalt path to the neolithic Coliseum, we were charged with energy. A New Year's Eve concert with any band is always fun. Dancing and celebrating another revolution around the sun is always a good time to meet girls and make friends. As we plod along in line, cracking deadhead jokes on our way to the front (how many deadheads does it take to screw in a lightbulb? None. They don't screw in lightbulbs, the screw in dirty sleeping bags), several bummed heads walk past us, dismayed at their misfortune.

"Fuckin' scalpers, man. Bullshit."

We look at our tickets.

"They're definitely the real deal, right?" I ask.

The efforts of The Grateful Dead's ticketing department had been elevated to a magical plateau for these exclusive New Year's Eve admissions. When you tear the ticket, a genuine ticket, purchased only through the group's own agency, the interior revealed glitter. They had somehow melded two materials together and adhered glitter flakes into the core, making a magic dust that, as one was ripped apart, immediately revealed the true value of the product. If genuine, it was handed back to you at the double doors surrounding the Coliseum, verifying your admission. The roar of a pre-show crowd inside was intoxicating.

Decades from now, I will still feel the pull of that deep, sonorous roar, a co-mingling of laughter, storytellers, vendors yelling "popcorn," the whole thing like it was five seconds ago. I can feel the energy, taste it on my tongue. It gets inside, begins to unwind in me, to mutate.

As we approach the doors, through the glass walls I see a long bank of pay phones hanging off their hooks, all spinning in space. This was how deadheads played the show for family and friends stuck on the East Coast: pay phones plugged with quarters, the band can be heard through the tinny, tiny speaker back in Newark or Raleigh, listening live through the speaker on their answering machines in a kitchen somewhere, dancing to the sound. Transferring the signal in the most inept, crazy way; these people are weird and clever. Closer and closer with our tickets, and then— no glitter.

"These are counterfeit, sir." A security staff member steps forward at those words.

At that time in the Dead's troubled fan history, kids like us were more than likely to bolt past the taker and launch ourselves into the thronging mass just beyond, free and clear for the night. This guy let us know in a look: *try it, motherfuckers.*

"Out. Next!"

We hang our heads and turn away, deflated at our denial to the year's biggest party. We walk down the winding asphalt path. But Jim, in his ever-stimulated nature, whips out a joint, lights it, and points to the massive, throbbing parking lot below—a carnival if ever there was one. Not having one thing demands another takes its place. Time is constant, and we need to be turned away by the gatekeepers, from time to time, if we are to live. There are thousands of people in this parking lot definitely not getting inside tonight. He puts his arm around me, making a sweeping gesture to the bustling marketplace beyond.

"Tonight, our show is the parking lots of Oakland. Let's go find some beers, baby!"

Twenty minutes later, I find myself pounding away in a group of twenty-plus drummers in a freezing parking lot in Oakland on New Year's Eve, an anarchic crowd of swirling ecstasy, a couple of girls in Siouxsie make up and black funeral dresses spinning slowly next to glaze-eyed kids in Guatemalan drug rugs and suburbanite escapees with whistles and suckers, dreadlocks and mohawks, leathers and sweaters, all swaying to the post-everything beat. Gigantic stalks of incense and sage burn, the smoky scene intense and primal. It's the New Church, the place where the new lost generation goes to find Gods and Goddesses, to be together in spirit and music, to share love and magic and sex and drugs. All is accepted, no judgments. The edge between the outside and the inside of these cultures is sharpening, and I'm on it, trying to keep my balance while the black hole continues to open.

I glance into the abyss, and there it is.

A tall dark-haired girl is smiling to herself, hippie skirt over blue jeans and battered blue Doc Martens, dancing like a dervish, her energy erratic and thick. Her hair seems to be several different distinct styles; a couple dreads with a shaved section and another, clear cuts to hold onto old notions? It is unique, weird, and distracting.

I've stepped in to play on some guy's giant conga and I'm watching the space all around her while trying to stay on beat with these maniacs, throwing quick glances at her sultry, magical form. Non-human vibes. She holds a bundle of burning sage, smoke swirling and circling her in ways that reminds me of fairy realms and primordial sensuality. Our drumming has reached a crescendo, and all are now making eye contact, the 'when to stop' look; this is not a song, it is a jam. My band would be ashamed of me. After fifteen minutes of intense pounding, we all need a break.

The guy who bangs metal sticks drops out first, then the two little reggae bongo dudes. That leaves a dozen of us rallying to greater heights and all intensely staring at each other. A giant with dreads to his knees takes the lead. We drop into deep driving triplets and in a last dramatic flourish someone lights a handful of bottle rockets that explode in the night sky as we end—BOOM BOOM BOOM! Suddenly it's over; arms floating in space. Everyone cheers. Jim smiles, squeezes my shoulder and laughs.

"Nice story, Nostradamus."

The girl approaches, never breaking eye contact. I cross my eyes and stick out my tongue, betting on cosmic goof. Suddenly, she leans in, and we make out in a way that's both scary and electric. I have no clue who, what this person is. That thing, though, the psychedelics bring your guard down thing, gets us right to business. Business tonight is tongues, flesh, and sweat. Those not lucky enough to get tickets to see the concert inside the stadium were making our own show outside.

"My name's Dawn," she whispers, staring deep into me. I'm nervous, reminded of things masquerading as human.

"Pleased to meet you," I reply, smiling and taking her hand respectfully, fully implying I'm going to kiss it, but I lick it instead. She laughs, a throaty, deep laugh that reminds me of a pirate who's just slain her sworn enemy.

"And you are?" she asks. I lean into dramatic exposition, as my imbibed nature dictates.

"I am known as the thief, the lie between believe, the skater, the dropout. The winner and the loser, at your service." My real name, something I've had to explain since forever.

"I love it," she says and licks my hand back.

A sandpaper tongue like a mongrel, up my hand and the length of my forearm. Immediate lovers for the evening, we abandon Jim, caught up in conversation with other revelers. He waves, points to his eye, as in *see you later*. I try and make a mental note about where his van is parked, then disappear.

Carousing among the makeshift circus that follows the band from state to state, row after row of bedazzled, wildly painted vehicles, hundreds of vehicles from dozens of towns and cities, we hold each other with an intensity that exposes our energy, our youth. Wide-eyed we wander among the buses and cars from all over, visiting with strangers from North Dakota and wild burrito makers from Maryland. We can't keep our hands off each other; a night full of opportunity.

A woman sitting on a cooler full of beers offers us two for five bucks, and we indulge. I catch sight of another bottle in the chest, half-hidden by melting ice.

"What's that?" I ask. She smiles.

"That, my friends, is five dollars a shot." She pulls the dark green bottle from the cold and holds it up. It has a label with a green dragon on it, nothing more. I pull Dawn closer to my side.

"We'll take two each." I hand over a twenty.

The woman's eyes are sneaky as she uncaps the bottle.

"Very well. But be warned: Here be Dragons."

I smile as Dawn shoots hers straight from the bottle, then me. The woman smiles, takes the bottle back.

"One bit of advice." She hands us our beers.

"If you find yourself on the edge of panic, or fear, remember, it's okay to freak out, just remember to freak back in." We laugh in full confidence, thank her for that advice, and disappear into the dying embers of the decade.

The night starts to become surreal, at war with reality. I'm caught off guard when I see a man in full doctor gear—white coat, stethoscope around the neck, clipboard—walk briskly by, in deep conversation with a couple of girls through the throngs of partygoers, and a young naked woman follows behind them pedaling an old bicycle, smiling at everyone. Mad distractions abound as we sink deeper into the night.

Doctor and girls continue walking, their background buzzes and shifts from parking lot to interior of a…hospital? I watch them disappear down the hospital hallway, a shimmer in time and space right there in the parking lot. Dawn laughs as she pulls me into the spring-loaded doorway of a massive old school bus. Into the night, and each other, we disappear.

INT. HOSPITAL HALLWAY- MORNING

Two girls, HANNAH and SHELBY, both 21, both in flowery
dresses and long, untamed hair, walk briskly with DR. HENRY,
45, stethoscope on neck and clipboard in hand, stern and
concerned.

> DOCTOR
>We can't release him until tests
>come back, they should be done this
>afternoon. And the police want to
>talk to him.

> HANNAH
>But you're holding him against his
>will, he's not--

> DOCTOR
>He's not conscious, and since you
>are not--

He looks them disapprovingly, shaking his head.

> DOCTOR (CONT'D)
>--family, you have no legal
>authority to take him. His
>condition is unstable, at best.

> SHELBY
>This place is not right for him,
>man. He needs fluids, real
>medicine.

> DOCTOR
>I assure you he is hydrated. What
>medicine, exactly, would you give
>him?

They pause as a nurse passes in the hall pushing a gurney
with a covered stiff.

> HANNAH
>He's an organic soul. Herbs are the
>answers to human problems, not mass-
>produced chemicals that only--

> DOCTOR
>If he was taking any herbs or
>supplements, we'll find out. His
>tests aren't back yet. Care to tell
>me what else might have been in his
>system?

Shelby and Hannah look at each other.

                    SHELBY
          We haven't seen him in days. Then
          he shows up hours ago, looking
          like, like--

                    DOCTOR
          Like what? Someone possessed? Is
          that what you were gonna say?

They all turn to reveal BILLY THE KID, 24, behind a glass
window in a hospital room behind them, bound to the bed,
struggling against his straps. Eyes closed, like a wraith in
bondage, slurring strange tones.

                    DOCTOR (CONT'D)
          It took four orderlies to take him
          down. Four. Tests are back soon.

                    HANNAH
          What's happening to him?

EXT. HOSPITAL- MORNING

The sun cracks the horizon, light across the lot.

INT. HOSPITAL HALLWAY- SAME

                    DOCTOR
          He's coming down. Angel dust maybe?
          PCP? Maybe LSD? You tell me.

The girls hold hands, watching him writhe beyond the glass.

                    SHELBY
          We only smoke pot.

Doctor smiles.

                    DOCTOR
          You only smoke pot. He's on I-don't-
          know-what. We'll find out. And
          those clothes lying there?

CLOSE UP on a pile of clothes near the bed. Shredded jeans
and T-shirt, all tattered and bloody, muddy sneakers.

                    HANNAH
          Omigod, is that blood?

                    DOCTOR
          Well, it aint ketchup. There's mud,
          weeds, bunch of candy wrappers in
          his pockets. Cops are coming to
          collect it all later. Evidence.

                    SHELBY
          Evidence of what?

                    DOCTOR
          I have no idea. But he's definitely
          been on the move.

They watch him continue to struggle.

                    SHELBY
          Is he hurt?

EXT. PLAYGROUND - SAME

Sun up, kids run everywhere.

                    DOCTOR (V.O.)
          Not a scratch.

EXT. PLAYGROUND- MOMENTS LATER

A little girl, 8, runs from the swing set to the jungle gym.
Seeing something on the ground, she stops and picks it up.
It's a ring on a human finger. She runs it over to her
mother, excited.

                    LITTLE GIRL
          Look what I found!

The woman drops her coffee, screams and drops the finger as
her daughter places it in her hand. A couple other mothers
gather to stare at the abandoned digit.

Young Native American girl ELLIE, 16, walks by, smiling at
the discomfort of the ladies and, seeing the object of their
disdain and horror, speaks up.

                    ELLIE
          Smell my finger...

Laughing at her own joke, she whistles an upbeat tune as she
walks away. Glares from the concerned citizens.

EXT. PINE FOREST -DUSK

An OLD MAN, race indiscernible, 80 or more, in tattered robes
stitched with feathers and dirty rags, hangs upside down high
up in a pine tree. Held in place by his knees swung over a
stout branch, he ties off a long piece of string, the bottom
tied to a large stone, dangling in space.

Above the stone on the string, hole drilled through to keep
it staring directly downward, is the upper half of a HUMAN
SKULL.

With the dexterity of a much younger man, he swings out his
knees, releasing, but instead of falling he lands feet first
on the trunk, defying gravity. He climbs downward, hands
first, feet above like a human spider, effortless. Hair
falling towards the earth along with his robes, he wears
nothing underneath. A wizened, ancient body.

5

ADAM IS TIRED of Texas. It's too big. He longs for something more intimate, more personal. He grows up racing: scooters, BMX and then the big-time. He plows into a neighbor's fence the first time he's on a motorcycle, almost losing his leg. His mother immediately makes him promise he'll never ride one again.

Promises and limbs broken again and again, he goes faster and higher, topping out on a 600cc run from the cops through a barbed wire fence up a hill, almost escaping but not quite, and then—he's in juvenile detention for a minute. While in juvenile hall, an older guard tells him something that sticks with him.

"Let what is happening teach you what wants to happen next."

Months later, he has an epiphany when his electrician father comments on how difficult it was to find a customer's house that day.

"You know what people need is some goddamn visible address numbers. Something you can see from the street." An escape plan is hatched that very evening.

He finds Jesus in 1984. Two years in, his youth pastor takes him to a Depeche Mode concert in Houston where someone slips Adam acid in a bottle of water. He watches, seemingly from outside himself, his strengthening connection to the Holy Spirit making his head screw on tighter, not looser. He can see it now—it's all beautiful. He makes it out okay, if by okay we're agreeing that when you decide in the middle of a Depeche Mode show on your first acid trip that your life should be lived on the road, not in a stifling, soul-sucking dwelling that drains you of all capital and humanity, then yeah—he's fine. Late one night, he jokingly calls the phone line of half-wit Evangelical Pastor Robert Tilton, a white-powdered, brushed wool staple of late-night TV across the south who promises financial success to those who donate in the next five minutes.

"This is Eve, who am I speaking with tonight?"

"Adam."

"Really?" she asks. "Yeah, it's me."

"Can't believe we're meeting on the phone. I read it differently." They both laugh.

Fullerton, 1987

EVE FINDS LIFE BORING because, like most bored kids, she's surrounded by boring people. No sparks, no jazz. There's the occasional goofy uncles or wacko siblings to get weird with, but, like Adam, she longs for something more. Outside of tagging along on her sister's weekly jaunts to bars, mod clubs and backyard BBQs, she figures that's just the way it is. Life is letting others tell you what to do.

Thank the Lord, she thinks, that she didn't marry that idiot boyfriend from high school. Dying of friendly fire in a Panamanian invasion was the last thing she wanted hanging over her life. If she'd married him as he wanted before he left for Latin America, she'd be alone, horribly alone. A twenty-two-year-old widower was not how she pictured herself, even if she didn't really know who exactly that "herself" person might turn out to be. As alone as she was right now, she sees a future for herself outside the cultural wasteland that is Southern California. Her options may be spare, but her eyes are wide. She's looking for it.

She likes to make people laugh; realizes she has a knack for it. She steals Richard Pryor and Red Foxx jokes off the albums she rents at the library, no one's the wiser, everyone believes she's just hilarious and clever. Emboldened by this, she memorizes dozens of one-liners, to the entertainment of her sister's friends, and even more brazenly never hesitates to cut someone down if it'll make her sister laugh. She specializes in the subtle art of the slam, her sister often joining in—a partnership in temperaments. Tough as leather but always alert to other anxieties, so as not to hurt anyone.

She gets a job answering phones for a company advertised as "Success-N-Life," taking calls from donors to the fortunes of a self-professed man of God who will soon find his finances the subject of multiple criminal investigations. Whatever, she thinks. She has a job, and it was the late-night call that made her laugh, and ultimately agree to a date, which ultimately led to a child. And what do you name the child of Adam and Eve? Eden. The road becomes their first home.

San Fernando Valley, 1988

LIGHTNING LOSES THE GIRL in a conflict over the guitar, grocery money all gone again, but it's always more than that. The fight was huge. Items hurled and smashed against inner and outer walls, residents of nearby yards flock to watch the carnage. Cops are called, no one's hurt, just loud and offensive for such a family neighborhood. They're both twenty-five. The swimming pool next door holds a bunch of kids celebrating a birthday, and the parents lament their children witnessing adults treating each other so poorly. It's suburbia—what can you do? Even the neighbors know: it's over. The girl leaves, the guitar remains.

That night, a rare thunderstorm lights up the San Fernando Valley, even going full Midwest on the scene and killing power throughout Reseda and Lake Balboa.

He gets a kick out of wild weather and being half Native American, finds truth in the voice of nature and when a bolt of lightning literally hits and torches his (admittedly piece of shit) Corvette in the driveway, he gets the point and takes the impractical but in the long run always better spiritual approach and leaves it all behind. Within a week he empties the house, sells it, quits his job, gets rid of the cars. He's taken the storm as an omen of positive change.

The following Wednesday, Summer Solstice, he walks, for the first time in ten years, east. Headed to the freeway to find his people with his only possessions, a backpack and the Fender. He will not abandon his true love, nor any opportunity to rock.

Guitar strapped around his neck, long black hair blowing in the breeze, he strums Black Sabbath's 'Paranoid' as he heads towards the on ramp out of there, forever. His whole life he was called Troy, a name he always disliked. Now he's Lightning. The neighbor kids blast a song he's never heard before as he walks out of the neighborhood, away from this life forever.

"Who is this?" he asks the punk white boys drinking beer in the front yard. He wants to remember this song, strumming along, it's the soundtrack to his next chapter.

"'Shake Your Rump' by the Beastie Boys."

He continues to the corner, *chick-a-chick-a-chick*-ing towards a new world order.

San Martín, 1989

ED DOESN'T MESS around. The opportunities after getting out of military prison are too vast, too beautiful, so he gets right down to it. Within a month of his release, he's got a girl, a dog, a Nash Metropolitan once owned by the midget king from The Wizard of Oz and a piece of soapstone the size of a football, ready to carve and find the vessels hidden inside, both of himself and the stone. He buys carving tools and wanders the highways and byways of the Southwest, a visit to a commune out in the high desert, working on music videos in Hollywood, participating in the best the world has to offer. He continually carves.

"What is this?" he thinks, the stone gradually changing shape, becoming, becoming. He is happily perplexed at its ability to resist being defined.

"What am I?" the stone thinks.

His power to generate positive energy bolstered by Adonis good looks and a kind, handsome face with blue eyes like the sea layered inside a ramshackle, hand-spun wizard cloak with dusty cowboy hat only strengthen his appeal to a certain segment of society, the beautiful ones, seeking out those different than themselves, never wanting to stop falling in love with the world. There are people, and there is magic in many of them. Magic gravitates to magic. He lands in incredible places with amazing humans, always willing to walk away. The girl departs quickly, then another. His commitment levels are, shall we say, unremarkable. No hard feelings, just another free moment. June of 1989 finds him in Camp Verde, Arizona. He has begun to see what's inside the stone.

Phoenix, 1989

DRIVING CABS PAYS Gilles' bills, barely. It works, and that's enough in the days of when just enough was good enough rather than a punishing struggle to keep one's head above water. Heather and Gilles meet in the break room of the Radio Cab offices on her first day. He's been driving for a couple years. They soon form an alliance based upon their mutual distain for corporate-speak, fake smiles, and anything but the darkest and bleakest of poetry. They love each other and are well into several tours of transporting Phoenix's best and worst citizens around the sprawling, crawling metropolis when they conclude: we can't do this all the time.

"It's too hot," was Heather's main complaint. Though an avowed nudist, she had to keep herself in clothes if she wanted to keep herself employed. She longs to be naked most days, even more so when the temperature jumped above ninety, which in Phoenix, happened earlier and earlier every year.

Gilles and Heather make a great team, always willing to learn from one another. He teaches her how to play guitar and fiddle, she takes him streaking for his first time at a music festival in Flagstaff. They escape into the woods after flashing their (admittedly, it has been said) generous genitalia, finding their stashed clothes and slipping into the hidden truck, laughing and bouncing away on a dirt road, far away from the abandoned pants and shirts on the field to the shock of country music fans across northern Arizona. They've got a story to tell.

Gilles takes her rock climbing in Utah and together they were finding a sort of perfect life together. Too perfect. They loved adventure, but what else is there? The shared apartment was getting stale. Music don't sit still for long.

Pico Rivera, 1988

SHE STARES ACROSS the Santa Ana freeway, sitting on her backpack and rolling a cigarette. Perilously close to the cars that enter the onramp which she has walked up, a tight turn against a concrete wall that allows for no love lost between woman and machine. In other words, no place to catch a ride. Here we find her, Easter morning, growing out a shaved head and trying to make a break. Walking away from one life and getting ready for the next is our theme here, so let's make brass.

Dawn was meant for dance, there's no doubt. She has all the moves, always spinning away on some tangent or twist. Dad dances, Mom dances, dancing is the thing, "it's all dance," she likes to say. But when push comes to shove, she's a leader, not a follower, and The Arhoolie Dance Collective of Santa Fe Springs already had its hierarchy in place, plus—it just wasn't her scene.

And so, in the dead of night, she packs up and walks away. Not sure what comes next, she tries to listen to the universe, a real task in the buzzing, droning urban landscape that is the Los Angeles basin. A lot of echo. Instead of listening to the trees and the birds for messages on the wind, she must interpret the song of the universe as it sings out of an old Dodge dart whirring past, sputtering as a way to explain the situation. She makes for the highway, chlorofluorocarbons on her mind.

After several hours of fruitless attention to the passing of lives, she sees it. Climbing the ramp, cutting the turn at a quickening pace, an old, multicolored school bus with bikes loaded on the roof, the type of ride that screams "We will pick anyone up." She jumps, seeing them before they see her, aware that, possibly, this is next. She laughs as she waves her arms. The bus rounds the turn and heads for the straightaway, gaining speed. There is no room to pull over anywhere, no way no how. There's literally three feet between the massive concrete wall and the white line that demarcates the Santa Ana.

At her elbow cars whiz past, staring at the girl they immediately judge as stupid for placing herself so close to mortal danger. They don't know her. She remembers Wilde: "All great ideas are dangerous." Seeing the trail of cars behind the school bus, it's clear: they're already pissing people off. The driver sees Dawn, pulling off her sunglasses, the sun blinding her as it rises over the concrete barrier and Easter Sunday breaks on the West Coast. Eve and Dawn make eye contact for the first time, both smiling.

Eve nods, *yes, I see you*, and waves her forward, like a quarterback, as in "go, start running." Dawn smiles and has her pack on in a flash. She runs with the flow of traffic as the ragged machine barrels down on her. Eve cranks the spring bolted door open like some gaping maw of old-world magic, pulling errant wanderers into it, an action scene from a never made movie. The bus slows down, but only slightly. Car horns blare from behind, making them both laugh as the opening to a new life matches her pace. She looks over and sees Eve, smiling, but eyes on the road.

"You gonna get on or what?" A Brillo-haired man in overalls steps into the breezeway, arms out. "Come on! You got it!"

Now at a sprint, Dawn glances quickly before she leaps left, into the waiting arms of a new world. She makes it easily (athletic, fast, and all that), and the door cranks closed as they gain speed, heading south. The sun has risen. Eve gets up to speed, shifting into high gear, cars buzzing around her, before she looks closely at Dawn, panting on the floor next to her. They look at each other, smiling.

"You could have run faster, ya know."

"You could learn how to drive, ya know."

They both laugh and high five. Instant attraction.

ARIZ ONA/ NEW MEX ICO

6

January 1

I TRY TO THINK as my eyes focus, forced to adjust. It is the most unnerving and strange thing if, still drugged and semiconscious, you awake in the back of a giant, gutted school bus, ancient in nature, looking up at a ceiling painted like some fucked up psychedelic Sistine Chapel but this one starring pigs with bat wings and strange oracle motifs, hanging plants swaying with the motion of the bus, whining in a 70-mile an hour wind, making the ceiling seem strange and far away. After a minute, confusion starts to dissipate, my mind starts to reassemble and readjust. I'm rattled and scared.

I seem to be on a battered transport that bears a slight resemblance to the Millennium Falcon, if the Falcon was on drugs, much more than a shuttle for schoolkids, quietly escaping the imperial guards of Oakland's urban jungles. Out of instinct, I reach out and find my skateboard, check my pockets. All intact and present. Never lose your board or your wallet. I sit up. We're passing through farmland, rain falls in light sheets in the distance, the sun's about to rise in the east. Dawn, asleep beside me, wears an oversized shirt that reads *My Life with the Thrill Kill Kult*.

Her knee is tucked into my crotch, still magnetized from the evening before. She is out like a light, and when I sit up, she swivels her head onto a pile of blankets, unaware of my existence. Is this her home? This vehicle is populated by who, exactly?

"Morning," says a voice from behind me.

I turn to see a Native American kid only a little older than me with long hair sitting on one of the only seats still in the bus, smoking a cigarette.

"You with Dawn?" He takes a drag off his cigarette.

"Yeah, yeah, I guess," I respond, unsure of my answer. He smiles.

"Welcome aboard." He leans over and shakes my hand. "Lightning."

I tell him mine, he seems skeptical. This from a guy who just introduced himself as Lightning.

"Yeah." I try to stand, but the bus sways and I sit back down. Lightning nods and turns back in his seat to look out the window, making it clear he's disinterested in more conversation. I look around at this passed-out group of itinerant travelers. It seems as if I'd been Shanghaied. Literally.

A good reason for not finishing college is being kidnapped, I guess. I have to stop this thing and get off. I don't belong here, there's been a mistake.

The hum of an ancient engine in high gear and assorted snores, barely audible chatter from behind a curtain at the back of the bus and a tinny, quiet country song escaping the driver's AM radio all bleed together and feels like an intergalactic cruise. There seems to be a lot of people along for this ride. Beds, bikes, and colorful blankets dominate the interior. I'm not hung over, I'm still drunk. It's a confusing first minute of consciousness. Be here now is what this now is.

I stand up and peek through the edge of a curtained window, draw it back slightly to see. Dream-like, I see no vehicles in either direction, both lanes open and empty, as many off ramps into who-knows-where are available for the choosing. Then, a tractor trailer passes us pulling two cargo trailers full of—garlic?

The car tailgating the garlic truck has a bumper sticker that reads 'madness takes its toll, please have exact change.' After writing my own chapter last night before dropping into the abyss, I chose monsters. Life suddenly feels weird and dangerous. Did I just have sex with the wicked witch of the west? I grab a water bottle rolling around on the floor and drink. It's warm and tastes like copper, but I've swallowed worse.

There's a lot to learn from the texts and teachings of American dropout culture. From Croatan to hippie van, the universe has a master plan that feeds on the souls of the willing. I grew up in a wrecking yard, so I knew characters—but this was something different.

A slight digression on what makes a "hippie bus," because that's exactly where the hell I've landed. Not my first choice, but not the worst one either. You've seen them out there, on the road to nowhere and everywhere all at once. Here's the details you missed by never getting with the program.

ORIGINAL RECIPE:

How the Universe Makes a Hippie School Bus

This method produces a beautiful hard shell outside and a tender and moist interior.

Ingredients:

(1) 1962 International Harvester School Bus

1. Take Harvester and run it into the ground across the landscape of Anytown, USA, for twenty years. Get at least 100k miles on it. Destroy any semblance of respect the vehicle has. Transport a thousand kids to school and back again, repeat a million times.

2. Spread thousands of farts, kisses, vomit and decades of laughter and urine spills around the interior of the vehicle, and make sure the psychic energy of a million schoolchildren's abandoned dreams and failed desires are rubbed into the interior, leaving no surface untouched. Make sure there's graffiti of only the most juvenile nature scrawled on the seats, walls, and ceiling, providing a mockery to our once-strong ideals of public education and a modicum of respect for authority. For that special touch, get some blood on the ceiling and floors.

3. When the bus no longer resembles anything good or worthy and is starting to shudder, write it off and dump it at the junk yard, call it death. Let the world go on without her, with weeds and invasive plants spawning not only through her undercarriage, but throughout the interior—her heart—as well.

4. Make sure rats, mice, and skunks live in her, and let them populate many years of their disease-bearing offspring

throughout the interior. For years. I can't emphasize this enough. Let bake in the desert sun and freeze in the winter nights for ten years, at least.

5. Take one medium-idealistic hippie kid, go to said junk yard of abandoned dreams on the outskirts of (insert town here), but only on the coldest weekend of the year. A good ten degrees works, but you can go as high as twenty. Make sure you are in desperate need and your new home, this ancient beast, needs to house at least eight people, immediately.

6. Come unprepared for a task as epic as raising the dead, so you have to borrow tools from someone who doesn't want to lend them. Be stoned, so your skill level drops to near grade school levels. Make it to the parts store ten minutes after they close so you can't order the parts you need until Monday (of course it's late Saturday), and you must wait another full day, sleeping in the shittiest hotel in the world just down the cracked asphalt road. Make sure the hotel is a name brand knock off, like Motel Seven. Spend Sunday smoking shitty dirt weed and watching the snow come down in drifts outside while a rambling preacher on AM radio drones on in the room next to you, all day long.

7. Monday comes and parts arrive. If you're lucky and talented enough, she starts. The engine turns over and you've got air in the tires, fluid in all the correct places, and miracle of miracles, it moves. Like an ancient beast that never thought she would be brought back to life, lives again. Life!

8. Rev engine. If she roars with approval, those of you that have been burdened with the task cheer. Scoop out of the ground and ease her out of her ancient bed of rock, mud, sleet and ice and into the junk yard driveway, idling.

Heat to 300°. If she sounds amazing, tear out all but two bench seats up front for people to sit on and talk your ear off while you drive. Serve at once. This bus will be the home of a group of amazing, beautiful and highly suspicious individuals for the next ten years. They will be the best years of their lives. None that live within her will ever forget her.

The school kids have long since drifted into obscurity and obedience, but this group will rise to meet the sun, and wander around, and share love, and be artists. It will all happen in the confines of her heart, so be sure and give her a good name, as these will be the happiest days of her life.

I can smell it now. Gilroy. As we speed through the garlic farmlands south of San Francisco, aromas reminding me of my current location in the universe, I approach the driver to ask questions about where I might find someone to answer for all this and what the hell is going on. Where are we? What is happening?

"Whoah! Who are you?"

He seems surprised to see me, a stranger in his home, but also a look that says, 'I've seen kids like you before.' We roll along what used to be called the 99, now it's the 101. Someday they'll probably change the number again, something they always do while we're sleeping, rearranging the world we move through. His eyes return dutifully to the road.

"Me Adam," and taps his chest. I do the same.

We laugh, both looking like cavemen up too late the night before and proceed to pick each other's brains.

"You with Dawn?"

"I guess? Is everyone going to ask me that?"

"Don't sweat it, she's been with us almost a year now. Everyone's fond of Dawn. You're an exception, she usually hates hippies."

"I'm not a hippie," I respond, bristling at the association, while also thinking to myself, *Jesus—do people think I'm a hippie?* Adam smiles at me in the mirror as he passes a tractor trailer, this one loaded with cattle. I learn they're heading to Arizona, by way of Salinas and King City. This is Steinbeck country.

"If you want out, I can drop you anywhere. I mean, sorry to abscond with you but I didn't see you. We're only about eighty miles out of the Bay Area though…"

I'm forced into an instant decision, something I'm horrible at. I can walk away, right now, get back to my life. A quick payphone call can put me back in my place. The same old narrative, straight to video. Something about this ride has a ring to it though. I don't know what it is, maybe it's the residual alcohol and drugs, but it's keeping my attention, rising up in me and edging a sharp reality into my mind that seconds ago was only a dream.

The sleeping passengers have a different energy, even while unconscious. Five, six adults. A child. Tapestries and old blankets cover the windows. A small table mounted behind the driver's seat has several mugs which I inspect as he talks and find they're attached to its surface by Velcro, so they won't spill while driving. Adam watches me tumble it over in my mind in the big rear-view mirror that for decades was used to monitor kids in the same way.

I'm at a crossroads, the universe giving me no advice whatsoever. A magical woman I had just spent the first night of the 90s with. A rambling dropout commune, an opportunity to get out of my comfortable nest and see. These are the people our parents warned us about. How bad could it be? I'll probably be home in a week or two, in time to salvage my school career.

"Sure, I'll stick around for a bit."

Adam smiles and we shake hands. He takes the last moments before the sun hits the horizon to clarify who they were, what they do and how it gets done. He explains in detail, as if training me.

The sunrise breaks the mountains and hits my face, shuttering my eyes and letting the dream machine of orchard trees influence me. I feel a connection with this place in space, an unfixed, speeding variable. As Adam shares the nuanced difficulties and freedoms that we will all take part in, it all seems cosmic in nature; a confluence in parallel narratives that somehow overlapped and drifted into my lane as I drift into theirs and now in real time, the predetermined writing, the girl, the shuttle to freedom.

I learn later that this is how all curb painters get trained. If Adam explains and you can't pick up what he's putting down, you're probably getting off the bus real soon. While the numbers he throws at me seem crazy, and I have no idea what he even means when he says, "curb painting," not even clear on what exactly we are going to be doing. My interview is over.

"Welcome aboard," he says. I've been conscious ten minutes. He asks me to roll a joint and I do. I suck at rolling, but I do it. I'm twenty-one, my first day as a curb painter.

I call Jim from a payphone in Needles, apologize for leaving him in the lurch, hang up. Call Mom, let her know I'm going to be gone for a while, don't panic, hang up. Call the lady who inherited the garage I live in, apologize and tell her she can toss everything. While she's yelling, hang up.

7

ON THE DRIVE to Arizona, I'm brought up to speed on this first family of great American curb painters. I've been jumped into the game. May I present to you:

Adam: Husband of Eve, father of Eden. Charismatic and bright, he seems to be all things to all beings. Need a book of 17th century poetry read to you beautifully? Done. Replace head gaskets? Easy. Make a four-course meal out of foods procured from a Safeway dumpster? Child's play.

Eve: Adam's partner, ruler of the roost. Beautiful, strawberry blonde and wise beyond her years. Won't hesitate to shut you down, often with the sharpest and funniest sarcasm that will remind you that she doesn't hate you, she just wants you to shut up and think. All the comedic timing I picked up from my old Steve Martin albums are alive in her.

Eden: Daughter of Adam and Eve, four years old. Precocious in the way only little kids are.

Ed: Poet and artist, with All-American Eagle Scout tossed in. Chronic stoner. Wild eyed and kind, the sage of the ride. He'll sketch a portrait of you when you're not paying attention, finding the magic in your spirit and bring it to the page.

Dawn: My captor and head dumpster diver for the family. She's a bright, six-foot tower, cloaked in blacks and greys, tied back braids of blonde, black and red, hovering like rainclouds and fog obscuring the magic within. A former circus kid, she's been on the road with this crew for over a year. An accomplished fiddle player and film freak, she's seen a thousand movies in a dozen languages. She talks to crows.

Lightning: Guitar shredder and organizer for the curb teams that bring in revenue. He is constantly playing folk, metal, country and rock on his old 1930s Martin guitar.

Gilles: Cab driver, mechanic and map keeper. Occasionally he'll disappear to teach cobb and adobe classes to get people to build their own homes out of renewable, less invasive materials.

Heather: Brewer that helped to re-open the Top of the Hill Brewery in San Francisco a couple years ago before catching this ride late last summer. She studied brewing with the masters in Bavaria.

I'm overwhelmed and intimidated. Does every one of them have to be so awesome? Next to them I feel basic, like I've just been born. What can I offer? A drummer and a skateboarder, I also build puppets. I hesitantly share this information, as it feels lame and embarrassing in comparison. They destroy that attitude quickly. These folks have no such hang ups about class and societal paradigms, and later that afternoon, as we pass a joint around, sitting in a circle in the back of the southbound vessel, sunlight tilting in through clouds of smoke colored light, they make it clear: they needed a skateboarder, they needed a drummer and a puppeteer. These are things they have little knowledge of or experience with. Now they have someone to teach them, like they will teach me how to play guitar, how to make adobe, how to disappear into the world. To them I'm not a novel addition, I've simply brought a different take on reality, a crucial variable that will allow them to, like myself, experience a bigger, more radical reality.

"Allow the picture in your head to be flexible, always," says Gilles, and grabbing his guitar he starts into a funky country song of his own design, "The Flexible, Sexable Bandit."

As intoxicating and magical as I find all this, however, they make it clear about the immediacy of the real world: we work hard, we make money. Work hard, party harder. I'm still in the dark about how and where and when we'd make money. I wonder if the term 'curb painting' is code for something else. Eve wants me to teach her how to skateboard.

"I hear you're a great skater," she says.

"Maybe," I say, and tell her when we find a ditch somewhere, I'll take her into it and teach her a thing or two. We laugh, both accepting the reference as crude but also genuine.

We try to paint address numbers in Flagstaff, but it's snowing. Weather called for clear skies, but they shrug it off and go south, as far as we can go without having to reprint our flyers in Spanish. The temperature climbs into the low 60s by the time we reach Douglas and the border.

It's weird to get let in on a thing that seems so secret, so smart and perfect that it could hide in plain sight. Curb painting was one of the great underground secrets of hidden economy and private culture, a last rush before the new world began.

Adam started painting addresses by himself in the mid-eighties and now, five years on, he's got a squad, his A-team. A crew of roustabouts that are willing to listen, ready to work, and always want to party. Armed with the simplest of tools—spray paint, reflective glass beads, stencils, bikes—they've been able to cut a path of financial freedom across the country. For some, literally years on end. No going home. No anchors.

Simplicity at its finest. You place a ¼ page flyer (four per page, economy) on every front door of entire neighborhoods. It was literally that simple. Ed decorated the flyer with some drawings of frogs and unicorns, but basically, that was it. When sending out magic messages, keep it simple and to the point so there's no confusion.

People were grateful for the service they provided, and often expressed their gratitude with a cold soda, some funny constructive criticisms as we spray painted away, or by sharing some leftover food they had, not wanting to waste.

NOTICE
LARGE REFLECTIVE

Address numbers are being painted on the curb. Your street will be worked on tomorrow. We are painting straight down the street to help patrol cars, deliverymen, ambulance, etc. better find your home. Statistics show that 78% of our homes are inadequately numbered for night use. We are using numbers that reflect brightly at night like highway signs.

The cost of this service is $8.00.

If you wish to participate, write your address number on the back of this flyer and place it in a window that is visible from the street.

Thank you,
The Curb Painters

The citizens of the homes we served ranged from the meek and mild Christians kind enough to chat with us while we collected our eight bucks, to the six-and-a-half-foot Navajo man in a three-piece leisure suit celebrating his birthday the day we appeared at his door and invited us in. We spent the next hour eating and drinking with his family, a peaceful afternoon with strangers no more.

We looked homeless, but in fact our homes were intact. A gigantic school bus, our place in the world, the stoop we retired to when the day was over. We live at campgrounds, some BLM land, or even a giant abandoned parking lot with a magic waterspout that, for the night, would serve as our offices, our bedrooms, our love shacks, our world headquarters.

We operated out of kindness and service, learning quickly that the real magic of the work was the delivery. That's true for a lot of things, but there was a real Zen-like perfection to this work that, if you owned it and lived it, was something special. Finding a personal methodology to the door to door lifestyle that was so far outside the mainstream, so different and weird, yet so professional and lucrative, was crucial. We must develop our own ways of doing things. I was writing in my head daily as we walked the streets of Anytown, USA. To do it just right, curb painting went down like this:

Day one:

In groups of two we walked down opposite sides of the street, putting our little flyers on every door of every house. No mail boxes. No, not ever. A federal offense, baby. When we approached a home, if there's a "no soliciting" notice, no flyer. Last thing we wanted was unnecessary confrontation. If there wasn't a sign, simply put a flyer on the door with a piece of tape and walk away. Not even a knock. Keep maps, wear watches to keep track of time. Walk all day. Highlight areas on the map you've worked so no one overlaps and meet up with others for lunch at a fast-food restaurant on the edge of the suburb to stay in touch, advise each other of potential problems as well as the overall vibe of the neighborhood. No pitch. If people were interested, they had no chance to get into a discussion with us of any kind. They wanted it, or they didn't. Eight bucks was a low enough number that few would balk, the service was real and immediate, and we delivered what we promised: Reflective address numbers.

Day two:

The longest day. On bicycles with baskets full of our supplies we start our shifts, streetside. Teams never start too early, we want to avoid as much distraction as possible, but early enough to paint what may be a hundred addresses that day. As soon as you see a number on yellow paper in the window, it's game on. Kickstands down.

Paint the background first. Solid white made tight and level by using painter's tape for a border. Sometimes you have to scrape the curb a bit with a wire brush, but generally this part of the country has tall, clean curbs. The aggregate they use is smooth down here, perfect for paint, and the weather almost always complies. You tape off the border, eyeing it because you must fit the address numbers inside. It's better to go big than small. Shake your money maker, hit it with the white. Let it dry for a minute before you apply the stencils. Now's a good time to double check your number in the window or wherever they hung the flyer. I haven't screwed this up (yet), but I'm told it happens more often than Adam likes. Getting stoned at nine in the morning before huffing paint fumes all day, I'm sure accidents are just around the corner.

We use cheap cardboard stencils to apply the numbers. They last for a remarkable amount of time, considering how much paint we cover them in and how poorly we care for our supplies. Press with one finger against the stencils to make the numbers clear and bright while spraying away with the other. We all have black fingers now, and Lightning and I discuss starting a band with this name.

Do not, under any circumstances, use too much paint. If it runs, it looks ridiculous and you have to do it again. Remember: we only charge eight bucks. Go slow, don't overdo it. There's no time for error or do overs. In my case, it helps that a few friends back home are talented taggers and I've come to curb painting with the knowledge they shared years ago about all this. What kind of nozzles to use, distance from target, speed of application, all of it. As kids we practiced on the shopping mall walls of our San Jose neighborhoods, unaware that I was learning job skills for the future.

And then, the reflective glass. The piéce de résistance. It glitters like a silver sea when shaken onto the quickly drying paint. We use cheap, dollar-store plastic saltshakers for the job. You apply the glass twice, once on the background, once on the numbers. The reflective glass beads are barely discernible from one angle, but from another? Shimmering magic.

We keep notebooks to record all the addresses we paint (after we're done in a town, once we've collected all our debts, the records are burned to avoid any possible tax questions). We work in groups of two: one to paint, other to the door. Cash only, miss. Five to ten minutes per house. Paid and gone. Most often they don't even come out and check our work. It doesn't matter though; our glittering numbers look fantastic.

Day three:
Follow up and try and collect from those who were not home to pay. A flyer on the door reminded them the work was done, payment was due, leave cash in an envelope on the door please. Everyone paid. You want real numbers; we always missed a couple of residents who went out of town or forgot and were out to the movies that night. But when you paint 200 curbs in a town and 97 percent pay, you're not gonna hang around for that last twenty-four bucks. We never stole, lied, or were rude or obnoxious. I think it blew people's minds that we were bold enough to do work of this nature, looking like we do. We're a proto-Burning Man animal cult of radicalized Americans, reveling in our wildness and freedom in the most natural of ways, dressing like weirdos most times, yet always able to look a homeowner in the eye and communicate clearly with them if they had questions or concerns.

If God created the world in seven days, Adam and Eve created ours in three. And that, dear reader, is how you become a curb painter.

Douglas, Arizona would seem, to lazy eyes, like any other sleepy border town. Upon reaching city hall, we're directed to the cool basement offices where we can pick up our peddler's permit, a simple, cheap variation on a traditional business license (no insurance required) that keeps us in the good graces of the cities whose curbs we paint. It's a steal at twenty bucks. Adam seems to have painted here before. I notice the office girls giggle behind filing cabinets and printers as they get us our paperwork. He's handsome, and it's clear they're talking about him, about us. I get it; we must really stand out against day after day of straight and narrow planners, construction guys. A steady stream of stable men come through looking exactly as society expects them too, the ready to stand in line folks, nothing more that permits and licenses for them. To them we must look like bandits escaped from a beatnik prison.

After helping set up camp in a local campground, Dawn and I walk down to the historic Gadsden Hotel to drink coffee in the lobby café with it's insane, fifty-foot stained-glass ceiling depicting desert landscapes, marble columns and chairs made to sink into and speak for hours about film. She's seen more movies than I have even heard of and is just as passionate. I feel overwhelmed and at a loss as to her references. I remind myself to rent more movies.

"A Woman Under the Influence by Cassavetes?"

Nope.

"Ivan the Terrible by Eisenstein?"

I digress, telling her I've seen Battleship Potemkin, which she dismisses with a wave. "Nah, first year film class stuff."

"Wild Strawberries by Bergman?"

No.

"La Strada by Fellini?"

No.

"The Passenger by Antonioni?"

"I've seen Two-Lane Blacktop—"

"It's okay, but mostly a snooze," Dawn says.

"Well, sorry it doesn't have a foreign director with a crazy name," I scoff.

She laughs, almost spilling her coffee. If this is how she operates, I'll turn the table, reverse the questioning, mimicking and imitating her, to her delight.

"Okay, you ready?" I ask, "for some serious cinematic grilling?"

She sneers. I'm nervous she'll have seen them all, but then the names all start to come back to me.

"Piranha?"

She rolls her eyes. "There's a movie called Piranha?"

"Damn right. 1980. I think it's written by John Sayles."

Rolls her eyes again.

"Sayles. What a hack." I continue, undeterred.

"Faust by Murneau?"

She shakes her head.

"Ha! 1926, *and* a German director!"

We both laugh, other guests at the Gadsden check us out, feigning interest.

"C.H.U.D.?"

No.

"Texas Chainsaw Massacre?"

She winces. "Ugh. No."

"The Hills Have Eyes?"

"Nope."

I've got her on the ropes, but I make a bad move.

"The Birds?"

"Of course! I've seen plenty of Hitchcock, it's all great." We rank about even, Horror and Foreign a steady tie between our cinematic histories, and we quickly pull back the curtain to expose the real meat and bones of our conversation: making our own films, telling our own stories. The subject of my screenwriting class comes up, and Dawn parks the conversation in the middle of our parallel ideas.

"You can write a script, why don't you write one now, while we literally have a captive cast and crew?" She sips her espresso.

I shrug.

"No, seriously. We could do this. You're in the world of active participation now." The thought of writing a movie and actually producing it on a whim is daunting and I like the idea but lack the confidence and try to think of other things, distracting myself. The fuse has been lit, however, burning towards a future explosion of our own design.

What kind of movie would I make?

"A horror movie, right?" She scoffs, slandering the possibilities of the genre.

"Horror is art too, you know," I respond, "and it has the same intentions as all great films: to make us understand the vitality of our humanness."

Our conversation is electric, animated in a way that now makes people watch us more seriously, like they want in, if only to know what it feels like to be as excited and enthusiastic as we are.

"We could use everyone in the crew, just write a script and get it going, I'll do the rest."

Dawn's confidence is contagious, and I find myself believing we could do it, make an actual feature film, on the back roads of America, on our own terms. I feel a thing rise up in me and begin to morph into hope, and the jazz from the bar, some post-bop sounding hard sax soloist fuels my excitement. I can tell she feels it too. She smiles, looking into the bar area where the trio of musicians are hitting their bridge.

"The score would be music like this," Dawn says, "only for a monster movie."

"Monster Jazz."

We recount as many road movies as we can. She has a deeper and more mature recollection of such things. Her list is incredible. Hungarian films. Agnes Varda films. Obscure and off-beat titles from around the world.

"My favorite though, is Wenders' Kings of the Road."

I tell her I've never seen or even heard of it, and then make a joke on the genre.

"Shot for shot, the best road movie—ever—is Cannonball Run." She laughs a beautiful laugh, a genuine laugh, like a rare bird alighting up and away from a tree. We hold hands as we walk back to the campground, a short hike through the heart of Douglas. A dry southwestern desert evening buzzes in my ears, a cinephile at my side, silent streets, so late that there's no cars now, and then the strains of a flamenco guitar float out a high window of the Gadsden.

I wonder—is this my Paris? I'm never going to live in those foreign, exotic places, and looking around, I think: why would I? Looking at the silver shimmers and desert panoramas, I feel it all move through me. I'm zooming in and out, seeing the Southwest as a magic landscape, the dry desert air, the way the stars sprinkle through the night sky, considering all contexts from old cowboy street corners to the universe and back.

There are moments in life when everything that has come before and everything ahead fades and the present crystallizes into a perfect feeling, a sort of dream state that was only a moment ago unrealizable, and then it hits. It rises up and overtakes you. It may last only a second or two, because those are the moments against which all future events in life may be compared. We search for this, confluences when the universe seems to be calling and saying "Hey, it's me—the Universe—I'm telling you about *you* right now. Listen." I'm hopelessly captivated. I can't wait to grab some spray paint and hit the streets. But first, some beers and a campfire.

We spend the remaining hours of the evening cutting our fliers and highlighting maps for each team of two to cover as much ground as possible. I was previously in the dark about how all this works. It's the doing that makes it all clear. Everyone is excited. They came north for the New Year, much farther north than usual, and the team hasn't painted in over three weeks. Cash reserves were running low, but now everyone seems confident we're about to head back into the black.

Next morning, we bolt like jackrabbits, taping fliers to every door we can. By lunch we're exhausted. Flyer day is the hardest. You never stop moving until you're out, and that can last well into the afternoon if you're hitting a neighborhood with big yards. We walk all day, except for Eve, who stays with Eden at the campground we'll live at for the next three days.

I'm happy to be included but remain a bit skeptical about the whole thing. A bunch of freaks walking the streets of small-town neighborhoods, painting their curbs and then going up to the door and asking for money? Cash? Someone's gonna call the cops or pull a gun. This was America. Arizona, New Mexico, and Texas account for more than 70 percent of gun ownership in this country. At least they would balk at giving us cash from their front door, right? That was my fear. I know how Americans react to strangers, and most of us, dressed like extras from a musical, had just distributed two thousand fliers to two thousand houses in the hope that our math plays out. We return to the campground at dusk, drained.

It was unbelievable. Piles of twenties, fives and tens, hundreds of singles, day after day after day. We usually earned several hundred a week, but, as I would find in the coming months, in places like San Antonio, we could easily hit the thousands. The best number Adam comes up with for actual returns is, I later learned, a business industry standard: an eight to ten percent return. Eight percent of two thousand (160) times eight (8) dollars equals one thousand, two hundred and eighty (1,280) dollars. Our overhead is food and gas, almost nothing in 1990. Gas hovers at eighty-five cents a gallon nationally.

That night in Douglas we have the years' first big fireside meet, a kind of weekly meeting. We clear grievances, make suggestions, pitch ideas for towns to paint next, etc. Passing a giant shell to clarify who gets to speak and who doesn't makes for comfortable conversations. The shell makes it to Lightning, and according to him, if all went according to plan, we would be in Maryland by March. Tickets to some Grateful Dead shows have been ordered, by him, and were waiting in a P.O. box in Dallas.

A collective sigh goes through the meeting, a hint that maybe not everyone is on board for another Dead show, especially one that lasts two weeks. That's good: the last people I'd want to get stuck with are the characters that dedicate their lives to the aging dinosaur known as The Grateful Dead. I must admit, the scene can be a blast—I wouldn't be here without it—but I often found the most dedicated followers to also be the most boring. It was a sort of steadfast clinging to a slowly dying fire, burning out, a kind of stereotyped 'what an outsider just does now' lifestyle, dragged and beaten through the 80s. And while the road is not for the weak or easily intimidated, listening to old Grateful Dead tapes and staying stoned all day in poorly maintained vehicles was, frankly, tedious and dull.

So now we have a bigger goal: East Coast in the dead of winter, a challenge that is not for the timid. I envision rivers of floating ice, snow-clogged places like Maryland and New York, a fever dream for a kid from California.

I speak up, daring to ask, "Do we have room?"

Adam responds. "If we find guys like you, then yeah—we need that."

Dawn and Ed smile, a glaring statement from Adam that I've made the first cut. Lightning chimes in, a deadhead to the end.

"This would be our treat for a good spring tour of our own."

Everyone looks around, unsure how to respond. Adam clears the air.

"Shit, we pull another month of good runs like this, we'll go to Paris for a week, fuck Maryland." Everyone laughs; Adam has lightened the mood and made it plain: we work hard, we get what we want. Dawn and I keep our idea of making a movie quiet; best not to rock the boat with crazily hatched ideas about becoming something else. If we can clear a thousand dollars a week for eight weeks, we'll be near ten grand and ready for the next phase.

'Next Phase' is a term I hear mentioned in whispers of conversations and so I kept my ears open, and my mouth shut. I buy a spiral-ringed notebook and rewrite my screenplay, adding elements of my new reality to the story. My brain is on overdrive walking endless neighborhoods, hanging flyers door to door, scribbling ideas for movies and lyrics for new bands yet created on assorted papers, receipts, and cardboard sheets. I wear myself out writing page after page to get to sleep so I can paint the next day.

I'm applying the lessons taught by my screenwriting teacher, Roger Margolis. He was a monster himself, chain smoking and pacing barefoot in front of the class, destroying my work in front of everyone, commenting on how much he loved my first draft and then it went to shit.

"What the hell happened?" he says. The class looks at me, relieved to see the spotlight focus somewhere else.

"I don't know, I..."

"Ah, you didn't try! You just gave us something to be interested in, then didn't do your work. You hooked us with your great pitch of a Native American kid becoming fascinated with the story of a coyote loose in New York City. That was great, you said so much right there, then you dropped the ball!" He's actually yelling, and my classmates seem genuinely horrified on my behalf.

"I'm still working on it," is all I can muster. He shakes his head, disappointed, walks to my desk and drops, literally, pages of notes that have forever served me in my work. I was so grateful he singled me out for attack. There's a grim satisfaction to be openly criticized in a group setting. It can make you better, harden you up for the world to come. We all need that, from time to time.

We hit six percent the first week, almost a thousand dollars in five days. We may be a dirty dropout cult, but we're rolling hard, loaded with cash, weirdo glitter freaks that you only see for a few minutes, on our knees street side, praying with spray paint cans blasting around little black and white clouds, cosmic goof graffiti artists, a sexy mix of denim, cotton, old mom jeans we've reconfigured in funky ways, tight shirts and loose skirts, slipping in and out of suburbanite reality in a moment, like a glimpse of some castaway cult. And when we hit you for eight bucks and then slip away into the deep Arizona night, we leave you feeling all glittery and good about yourself, pleased with our services. Occasionally, wanting to see the work, some homeowner will test us, eager to prove we're a scam, or cheats. We delight in these moments.

"Come on out," says Ed. He walks the skeptic homeowner to the street, knowing it's true; they can't see the work we've supposedly done when we approach the door to collect. He's proud to show them the finished product; a sharp white background, glittery and gleaming, against stark black numbers that stand tall, infused with the glassy effect that our beads have created, making the whole idea, once it's finished and being presented as a true work of art, feel like a true gift from us to you.

"That'll be eight bucks, sir."

We always shake hands and make eye contact. It's like our parents taught us, be polite and do good work. It's also like Cheech and Chong taught us: joints for breakfast.

Of course, not everyone is good at stencil work or talking to strangers or sprinkling glass across surfaces uniformly or a dozen other variables, things that all feel second nature to me. Adam's rule is hard and fast, you're in or you're out. While you don't have to be an extrovert, it helps. We're getting lean and muscular from our work (twenty-five push-ups at every curb keeps our spirits high) and our language poetic and thoughtful in conversations. Even when we're high in body, we're spiritual and clean in our thinking thanks to our constant physical exertions and positive exhortations to each other, and after the first hot run across the southern border (Bisbee, Douglas, Sierra Vista) we hit the first wall: City officials, with cops in tow.

Tucson is a bust because we hit a neighborhood that had already been singled out for curb painting by the Boy Scouts. Rule of thumb: Don't mess with civic groups. Boy Scouts, Girl Scouts, Freemasons, Elks—let them do their thing. They're good groups and, as civic-minded organizations, they're definitely capable of dropping a dime and getting you kicked out of town if you don't follow their rules. Tucson the beautiful. Don't mess with Scouts.

8

DOUGLAS, ARIZONA to Las Cruces, New Mexico. Somehow, over time, curb painters have cultivated loose connections to each other around the country. Numbers and addresses scratched on campground bulletin boards are considered lifelines, sometimes the only contact to other teams of painters, crucial lines when the numbers get too high and there's a quick need for a few reliable, extra players. Suburbs are blowing up across the Southwest in the spring of 1990 and without another couple trustworthy painters to roll with us on the bigger towns, we can't do it all. We often need a bigger crew for cities growing this fast. Staying put in one town for too long can have disastrous consequences; best to hit it and quit it.

"Some places, though, you just want to stick around," says Eve one evening.

We sit on the roof of the bus smoking cigarettes as she unfolds her massive, heavily marked up map of the entire Southwest. Once a gas station handout, her chart now looks like something more from Tolkien's Middle Earth, if it was made by Basquiat. The borders have been densely decorated with animal scribbles of every color, and a variety of markups and highlights in multiple colors of suburbs not yet finished but circled and highlighted as *ready by spring of '92*, or a town circled in black sharpie labeled *"mean cops,"* make Eve's map the most serious of tools in the curb painter's chest. From East Texas all the way to Southern California, these guys know the hot spots, the up-and-coming construction sites, the hidden hot springs, the free campgrounds and the best dumpsters to scavenge food and clothes from. Her map is a laundry list of how to do America right.

Pay phones, once found at every campground in America, are our tethers to the outside world. Adam hears the phone one night, runs over to take the call and pow—we're on the road. A tip has come in from East Texas (a guy named Atlas, of course), and Adam deadheads the ship to Houston, a short 12-hour drive away, for some quick curb runs into brand-new, previously undiscovered housing developments. Gilles and Heather stay put with the Econoline we just purchased and scout the rest of Otero County and southern Colorado for new developments. We make it across Texas overnight and jump right in, joining a team from Colorado for a couple weeks, suddenly the spot to hit, cash coming in at a steady pour. The third night there, in a spontaneous moment, Dawn, Heather, and I catch the band Ministry doing their industrial/punk thing at a club in downtown Houston.

If you didn't have your own scene, or weren't born yet, or just plain couldn't be bothered, know this: the scenes across the U.S. in those days, it's fair to say, were the best since the late 60s in terms of crazy kids, musical insanity, and straight up camaraderie. Anywhere you went in the country, east to west and north to south, the music of a nation was alive. Punk, Metal, Techno, Rap, Goth, Ska, Industrial and Hip-Hop—everyone was in the pool. We even threw in the furniture so you could sink to the bottom and relax in style in a drowning world.

Ministry, definitely the best of a new wave of industrial bands grinding into the 90s, made trouble seem effortless. The band loved attention, even when it was their lead singer getting punched in the face. If you want to get beat down and knocked out, Houston's your town.

Punk shows have pits, but this one was downright dangerous, a combination of drunken posturing and venomous shouting matches. Texans love slam dancing, but the truth is, implied violence aside, mosh pits rarely hurt anyone. If one goes down in a pit there are instantly a dozen sweaty hands to pull you back up and return you to the fray. Giant, swirling circles of people skanking, dancing, pogoing, and always with our arms around each other. The stage is wrapped in fencing, like country bands of old, but halfway through the show, in a poorly inspired moment one drunken maniac climbs the chain links, punches lead singer Al Jourgensen in the face and attempts to rip down the fence, ensuring the wrath of security and band members. Most of the crowd flees as cops enter the now brightly lit club, show's over.

Heather, Dawn, and I immediately start pounding abandoned drinks at the bar, all of mixed quantity and quality and then we're dragging Heather away from the guy who can't stop talking about his favorite bands as one cop blares out to anyone left who'll listen.

"This is now an unlawful assembly. Anyone who remains will be arrested and taken to jail." We escape into the night, laughing.

Four weeks fly by, just like that. We say our goodbyes to the Colorado crew and head back west, promising we'll call them if we catch any full sails. We pick up a couple hitchhikers in early February, but they last less than a week. It's true: some people just hate work. They want the benefits and will do their best to stay with crews like this, but Adam and Eve's policy wasn't just a philosophy: work hard or get out. We dump them at a gas station and wish them the best. We head straight for the gutters of Gallup. Spring has sprung. And then, who wouldn't love to work hard for a month then take a week off?

We descend on Verde Hot Springs early on a Monday, right when everyone's leaving, winding down the long twenty-mile dirt road that leads up and down across a desert landscape that runs from canyons and deadly drop-offs to vast unspoiled plateaus. Heather and I sit together at the back of the bus as Adam slowly navigates the bumpy road, Lightning and Dawn now up on the roof, pirates scouting for shore. We stare out the window.

"It always reminds me of Road Runner and Coyote out here."

Those simple cartoons somehow captured the deep, endless hues of immaculate terrain that we now pass through. There's a deep sense of connection the further in we go, feeling as if I'm being ingested by an untainted, glorious wilderness.

Everyone seems to have been here before, it's a destination that feels like a return, a magical place that everyone in the Southwest seems to know about, either by word or by herd, and all are excited when we find out Adam is steering towards it again. We're disappearing into a world looking exactly like it has for thousands of years. You feel it deep inside, a sense of something outside of country or nation. Just a place in time, unmolested and undisturbed. We've worked hard and painted so many address numbers on curbs that Adam has decided we'd take a week and chill out. Good idea.

We pass several campers and weekend warriors on their way back to civilization, pausing roadside with one family on their way out to catch the news from the road ahead: massive, axle-busting potholes to watch for, a water spigot at the trailhead that is clean and pure, we'll have to cross the river back and forth several times from the campground to get to the springs as the water is still high, caution advised. Sun still high in the sky, we arrive at a BLM-maintained camp. Excitement spreads amongst all as we immediately hit the trail, shedding our clothes and hiking naked, eager for a soak in the legend.

It's an incredible place, full of power and energy. Desolation and silence rule out here, no one for miles. The pools are carved into the mountainside. The hottest pool at the top cascades into the river below. One of the two pools is completely enclosed, cut out of the hillside itself with an arch as an entry and the low shelf carved along the inside is layered with candles. This place is the product of endless parties, trysts and storytelling, decades upon decades of magic locked into time and frozen in wax. Ed decides he's going to paint the entire wall in a mandala of some sort. His last dumpster score in Tucson was at a Michael's craft store, where he pulled out a giant collection of expired oil paints and brushes.

The day passes, sun crossing into shadow, and we eventually pack out, clothes back on. We make our way back to camp, a long line of whistling, wandering curb painters, up and down the little dusty paths that fork through the desert canyons, ravenous now and high on nothing more illicit than the way in which desert days can take you and launch your thoughts into the stratosphere, reeling and rolling to the onset of moonlit desert nights and conversations about the origins of desert features, of time.

As I kick little dust clouds I wander in thought, the brain thinking about the brain, that primordial ooze, once thick with miseducation and civilized, old model ways of seeing, reacting and responding. It all starts to thin and drain out of the cortex of thought, and as my newborn exposure to wildness unwinds decades of conditioning, in this newest state of myself I feel the drip fill the new well, letting the growth spread and capture the oldest parts of me and create a metamorphosis that is at once frightening and intoxicating. It's better than drugs, better than sex, better than anything I've ever imagined, an escape into the new me. I'm watching and wondering what happens to the mind when stars as multiplied as these, a number like a hundred million not seeming like an exaggeration at all, come out and find a place to play in the vortex of the age, a new age. Out here, and late into the witching hour, it always comes back to one thing: spaceships and aliens.

Everyone in the Southwest seems to have a UFO story. Later, after a dinner of franks and beans, Dawn and I go for a moonlight hike, stumbling among rocks and cacti. We wander uphill, climbing out of a small canyon and break out onto a ledge with a stunning view of a moonlit desert, angles and avenues of primordiality that give way to endless vanishing points and suddenly: oddball lights out of the far distance. It's too easy, too cliché.

"Do you see those lights?" Dawn points them out, and hesitant as I am to admit, it's true: they're weird and they're real. And now, away they shoot into the upper atmosphere, clicking and jumping around, impossible distances in no time, we sit in fascination and point to each strategic movement.

"You see that one?" I ask Dawn, just to verify the thing I think we're seeing is not some psychosomatic vision. Strange sightings are often written off as the result of too much stress or anxiety, but I've never been less stressed or more relaxed in my whole life. These are actual machines, ships moving around in what seem to be impossible speeds, and the light in them is incandescent, a kind of eerie, back-lit blue, a shimmering from within. Living discs, not of this world. And when they suddenly disappear, we laugh. We drink the last of our stashed forty of beer and make out on hard uncomfortable rocks. Covered in desert dust and sweat, we stagger back to camp as the moon slips back to the edge of the horizon.

Slowly, we work our way east. Curbs in New Mexico, then Texas. Glitter is the term we use for the glass, putting an art angle on everything we do, glitter—the herpes of the craft world. It looks like Epsom salts, but in fact they're very fine glass particles. Real world application, these are the beads body shops use for sandblasting car parts before priming and painting, back when America actually repaired stuff and didn't just farm everything out to insurance adjusters and new, made in China cheap-ass fenders and doors.

That damn glass though—it gets everywhere. It's incredibly difficult to wash off, fine like sand and our hands look as if dipped in glittery magic for a close up of a wizard's hands in some fantasy film or fairy tale where fingers deliver miracles and curses. The stuff inevitably becomes annoying and difficult to get off, making one a bit standoffish. It's glass, after all, and it cuts and mutilates your skin, if only in tiny terrible ways. We are constantly embedding ourselves with layers of it, and it's painful. We go days without removal, and it really starts to hurt. But there are lots of products and techniques, and everyone's got their favorites. For me, I wrap little strips of duct tape around my fingers before I start the day. Clean hands are needed when sleeping with a woman who likes digits.

On some days Ed and I wear the fancy western collar shirts we found for a buck apiece at a yard sale and tuck them in to our similarly cheap slacks and used cowboy boots, attempting to avoid attention as we were often high and sometimes tripping, yet always calm and collected enough to walk up to anyone's door and ask for payment for services rendered.

Our returns are now hovering near ten percent, and we decide that we can cut and run on the last couple weeks and catch a few extra Dead shows in the Northeast. We turn north and head towards the cold rain and snow of Maryland in March. The one thing I didn't want to do is coming to pass: going on Dead tour.

9

SAY WHAT YOU WANT about the Grateful Dead. The smell of their touring fans, the psychic stench of the mental landscapes that swirled around them, but if you were never there it would be impossible to truly explain the truth of it all, to understand the way their years went, show after show and tour after tour, avoiding mainstream culture and being so far ahead of the curve in so many respects. Thrift store clothes, co-op grocery stores, foods grown without GMOs, folk revivals, email and file-sharing communication going all the way back. Boycotting styrofoam cups and CFCs, how to make your own soaps and plant-based medicines, hemp clothes, reggae, all of it. I learn about the depth to which counterculture digresses from capitalist culture one day by asking Eve.

"Why don't you shave your legs?"

"Because razors are made by Gillette and they experiment on animals with their products, which I don't support. If you disagree with something, you don't support it. Right?"

And the list of things that hippies were hip to before the corporations caught on and branded it and made it all seem cool with lifestyle packaging and jacked up prices goes ever on. It's impossible to give the real dope on this scene, but I'll share what I recall. Here I am, stranded far from home in an ancient vessel chugging east to catch up with that motley gang of outsiders, monsters of the living Dead, a clan that by 1989 has grown far too big in number to ignore.

Thanks to the desires of our most capable painters, plus concert tickets and the promise of a two-week break, we leave the Southwest and head north. Gas prices go down the further east we get, the weather promises to not be totally disastrous, and we all admit that the tribe slowly gaining steam from all points America to congregate in Maryland for this tour were, in one way or another, our people.

On the road over the last twenty-four hours, passing through Missouri, Kentucky and Virginia, we met folks at gas stations, rest stops, and diners across America that are also going to these shows. Fans that are punks, nerds, cowboys and cowgirls, outsider artists and even semi-pro athletes, back in the minors for a tour. Winners and losers all, we're a congregation on a quick, thousand-mile journey. Luckily, we scored a quarter pound of weed in New Mexico as we headed out.

A complete tour in these drugged out days is mostly propped up and run by crappy, unreliable vehicles with even more unreliable captains. Pedal to the metal, coast to coast, thousands of miles in the span of two or three weeks is an insanely grueling experience. It's even worse when you're constantly high or surrounded by people who for the love of Christ won't stop listening to those awful bootleg cassettes that always sound like they were recorded by people as high as the people you're traveling with. A real, honest-to-God Grateful Dead tour, as opposed to a single show in your hometown, is a totally different beast.

First, you need people you can trust. When you're living on the road, you need to be wary of the people who are constantly too high and drunk that they can't make it back to the vehicle in time so you can't leave town. Those who must be sought out and thrown on board so the ship can part the harbor should probably be left behind. What'll happen if you *don't* leave them is eventually, they'll break down, mentally and/or physically ("oh! I hurt my back!"), and you'll have to go back, take them to their mom's house in Tulare or whatever, separating yourself from the tribe, or the tour, or whatever other trip you were on, caring for some grown-ass adult who can't handle their drink or drug.

Do not tour with these people. They may be super funny, or cute, or entertaining, but I speak from experience: do not take them along. It's not their fault. For their own sake leave them behind, let them catch a party or two in their home state and call it good. Leave the road to the real maniacs.

In the world of road tours, I've learned to keep close to the 'I've got my shit together' folk. It's an added bonus if they like to party, but generally they keep that kinda thing to a minimum. You know these cats, always the bootstrapping individual who, while also an excellent team player, can also go rogue and disappear, even if they're traveling with you, and will show up at the next show three states over. They'll make it, some way or the other, usually with new friends in tow and not be upset in any way. True road dogs.

Beware the others; the ones who must be found, picked up and watched over as their psychic armor hasn't quite, shall we say, come in yet. For some, it never does. Floating from town to town on a rock band's frenetic tour schedule, especially in the east, in winter, is a roll of the dice. There's a strong history of spiritual travelers, hoboes, mendicants and wanderers in American history, some predating the white man by centuries. Even today, folks from all over the world come here just to wander. Some walk. Some hitch-hike. Some spend eighty thousand dollars on giant, planet-choking motorhomes, and only scratch the surface of the thing they're looking for, but the motivation's the same: people looking for a new world.

When traveling anywhere in 1990, everything is cash-money-brother. Unfortunately, cash is easily stolen, especially when driving great distances every day, often high or drunk and with runaways, hitchhikers and hangers-on of dubious character. Debit cards were virtually nonexistent, and reliability on "funds available" varied wildly from state to state, usually firmly in the financial realm that goes from "no" to "none." Plus, cards are trackable. Always be a little paranoid while on tour. It's okay to freak out, just remember to freak back in. You've got to be in control. Or at least, someone does.

10

ADAM WAS BOSS, captain, shepherd, and parent in every conceivable capacity and was never out of it or absent for anyone's freak out session, of which there were more than a couple. He always held the reins, and every touring team needs an Adam and Eve. Those two shared controls of our family and reveled in it. And while there was a sense that it could turn into a power trip at any time, it's a model of successful living so far. It's their world, we just live in it.

The weather and the hostile urban environments of places like Hartford, Connecticut and Uniondale, New York are intense as we are coming straight off desert time and warm winter nights. Heat doesn't stay long in a gigantic vehicle with most of its interior stripped out to make room for sleeping areas. School buses are built as transport vehicles, not homes. We huddle together under piles of blankets that rarely kept us asleep for long when it's twenty degrees outside.

As we head into the storm, just south of Charlotte, North Carolina, we hit a thrift store for more socks, blankets, and heavy jackets, a necessity for a gang of people mostly in shorts, sandals and sweatshirts. As a bonus, I score a bunch of blues cassettes and a new AM/FM cassette player for the bus.

In a great comedic moment, Lightning and I have to install it as Eve drives, a ridiculous feat but when you've got ground to cover and the band is two hours from hitting the stage, you can't wait for a tape deck to be put in. When we finish and pop in Sabbath's War Pigs, the bus goes wild and turns into a dance party right there, doing seventy down the interstate. I glance out the window as we all boogie and see people in other cars staring at us, utterly confused or smiling. We're on tour.

Rain precedes the snow, and mud is tracked in with such regularity that our ride became known as the mud hut. Our crew picks up new members and soon we find ourselves in Landover, Maryland, home of the Capital Centre. We pack into a parking lot swollen with rabid fans. Punishingly cold rain keeps everyone's heads down, and our bus has now swollen to almost twenty characters. We dump a few, pick up a few more then on to the next show. It's frantic, it's cold and it's a bit crazy with all the snow and ice and dope and girls and dogs and kids and veggie burritos and glass pipes and chai (what the hell is chai?) and tie-dye guys and scammers and narcs and cops and finger pointing and late-night parties and nitrous balloons and yelling and lack of sleep and coffee and picking up trash in stadium parking lots as a favor to the band's reputation.

I get into one show. A chance to dance with twenty thousand strangers is fun, and when the audience feels it, the bands feeds on that energy, or so it seems as I blaze through the most acid I've ever eaten in a week. According to longtime fans of the band, this tour is a real run for the ages, a kind of world series-like event that they claim will be talked about for years. I doubt that, only because most deadheads seem to think every show is amazing and golden, every moment of every concert, and that is most definitely not the case.

Then, suddenly, two weeks later, we're in Atlanta and it's over. Adam, in a real Alpha moment at three in the morning, announces to a bus full of dirty hippies and an extra dog or two, at top volume:

"Everyone who is not willing to work their asses off for the next six months, kindly get the fuck off my bus!" To emphasize this, he punches the roof of the bus repeatedly as he speaks. We're parked on the outskirts of a giant Kmart parking lot, and our remaining stragglers head for the bank of payphones near the front doors of the monolithic superstore, heading for another ride, another way. We watch them walk away into a rare snowy night on the outskirts of Atlanta. Tour's over, kids.

EXT. FOREST WINDS DEVELOPMENT - EARLY MORNING

A developer in slacks and rolled up sleeves, GLEN, walks with head contractor SCOTT on the Desert Winds project, a gated, exclusive community, down the first paved street towards a collection of developing homes, all in framing stages. A dozen or so men perform various tasks on the homes.

> GLEN
> I don't see how the ground can be
> that solid. Just rock? The studies
> show water for sure. Do we need a
> bigger rig?

> SCOTT
> Maybe. I can show you the readings
> from the unit. Come on.

They walk towards a giant drilling rig settled into the earth a hundred yards away. As they cross the field, they come upon a man shredded into a dozen pieces, flies managing a steady, buzzing swarm.

> SCOTT (CONT'D)
> Jesus christ!

> GLEN
> Oh fucking god! What *is* that?

CLOSE UP on human corpse, desiccated and raw in the early sun. The parts are all there, they're just...separate. As if to add insult to injury, the torso has a T-shirt that is still readable: 'Down with development - keep the Sonoran desert wild!'

Scott looks at Glen, rubs his eyes, the onset of a headache that's going to last a while.

INT. SMALL TOWN POLICE STATION - LATER

An assembly of 5-7 officers, along with two FBI-types, PETE and KEN, sit in a darkened room watching a series of slides of shredded torsos. The one from the previous scene, plus a young girl and an old man. All are gruesome. Police chief LIPP, 40 with a shop broom mustache, turns on the lights.

> LIPP
> Looks like we're gonna have to hold
> up this project for a minute. This
> calls for--

                    PETE
              (standing up)
         We're not dealing with run of the
         mill murders here, boys. Whoever
         cut these folks up had a brutal
         fascination with carnage. They
         revel in it.

A woman's howl, wolf-like, from somewhere nearby turns all
their heads. They go to the back door of the room and open
it.

EXT. STREET - DAY - SAME

'Smell my finger' joker Ellie from previous scene, long black
hair and tie dye t-shirt with psychedelic leggings, walks
down the street, howling into a large MEGAPHONE. She stops,
looks over at the officers watching her, points her megaphone
and howls directly at them.

All confused, they return to the door and close it.

INT. POLICE STATION - SAME

                    PETE
         As I was saying, as of today we're
         taking over this case. The deaths
         are considered connected, not only
         to each other but to that
         construction site.

KEN, 25, clean cut fed, walks to the screen where the slides
are still projected.

                    KEN
         We appreciate your help and will do
         what we can to stay out of your
         way.

Murmurs and grumbles from the local cops.

                    KEN (CONT'D)
         We know this is a sensitive case,
         so let's work together to find this
         killer, okay?

He stares at the last slide, the vivisected torso.

11

APRIL ARRIVES, a full moon sale at a Kinko's reminding us to stock up on reams of sunburst yellow flyer paper to keep up with the curbs of gold. We wade deep into new housing developments springing up across the Southwest.

Our team now includes two crucial additions: Fred, a former New York City construction worker with the build of an athlete and giant dreadlocks. Any image you can conjure of a big city, skyscraper welder? This guy is the mental opposite. A published poet and the sole professional artist among us, he talks about the concept of temporary autonomous zones, a theory posited by Hakim Bey, some 'weirdo, post-beat cat' who Fred knows from poetry readings at some café back home. Fred describes Bey's theory, basically, as a "socio-political tactic of creating temporary spaces in the modern context that avoid and elude formalized structures of control now so prevalent in our modern, western world."

This thing he's describing, this concept of man's vision of a post-modern utopia is here, happening in real time in the Southwest. We listen to him describe the very thing we're now doing, the way we're living and how we're doing it, and he agrees. He came out west to find it, and here we are.

The first time he joins us around the campfire with his tour partner Morgan, he talks about various examples of temporary spaces in time throughout history, the human need to thrive and create a world of their own, if only for a time. He's right. We're living on the edge, and it is the correct edge. Adam questions Fred about all this even more.

"So, these theoretical ideas that your friend has developed are something we're living out, in real time, right here right now, right?"

Fred smiles as the campfire crackles and Adam hangs on his every word, nodding his head.

"It's true. The best way to create a non-hierarchical system of social relationships is to concentrate on the present and on releasing one's own mind from the controlling mechanisms that have been previously imposed on it." Fred always talks like this, and it's encouraging, if a little hard to grasp. I'm learning how to absorb higher thinking. Silence lingers for a moment, Adam chewing on this as Eve chips a question into the conversation, curious.

"But hasn't the whole of human history been full of such scenarios? I mean, we're just the latest incarnation. Right?" She rolls a joint as she speaks.

"Sure, but this time feels different, doesn't it?" He accepts the lit joint from her, puffs and passes. "Everything is becoming increasingly mediated. The millennium is coming, and never before has society been so divided and driven by opposing forces, market forces and military forces, even from within individual countries. It speaks to the general malaise that is only now settling down over the whole of humanity, a fog of compliance across all economic stages and peoples of this planet. Autonomous zones are going to be considered essential in the near future." Eve hits the circling joint and passes it, her exhale of pot smoke infusing her words.

"So, the thesis is, I suppose, partly that humans lining the road to future need the extreme solace offered by the primal energy of the desert and its inhuman sources to survive, yeah?"

"Kinda. Not just to survive, but thrive…"

Conversations like this are a real pleasure. I love information, even more so when it flies in the face of what I consider to be everything I've ever known as real, or true. As an added bonus, Fred's work ethic beats us all and allows him to go at his own pace, out ahead of us and often first back to camp, always kicking in a couple extra bucks of his own for a little bit better brand of whiskey, or beer.

His partner Morgan is a scrappy Connecticut woman who wants nothing more than to get away from her crazy born-again family and head out west. Also with a firecracker work ethic, once she's up to speed on curb painting, she leads the pack in the steady stencil category. Every curb she tags, perfect. Permanently caffeinated, she has an answer the second you've finished talking and it's usually hilarious. Between her, Dawn and Eve, the three amigas hit it off fabulously. Snappy sarcasm and asymmetrical anecdotes between the girls keeps the bar high. Heather has a smart collection of mechanic tools and the knowledge to back her sisters up; a gearhead looking more like a Mad Max extra than an escaped, on the run Christian who also cuts and dyes her own hair.

We've got a team that would make other crews shudder with jealousy.

And they're out there. Various loose-knit communities of curb painters—mostly strung across the Southwest but here and there across the nation—can pop up, not always allies. We're now officially a flotilla, waging war against complacency, stagnation, and rigidity, sailing into the great wide expanse of America. I'm now allowed to captain the ship occasionally, and I love driving the old bus, window down, wind in my face, listening to cassettes of old folk bands from Europe I bought for a quarter at a Tucson library. There are no shadows where we roam. My collection of sounds and ideas is growing.

The nineties quickly bring on the global warming news. Thanks to media coverage of that and a tanking CFC market, spray paint—the kind we use for painting curbs—is down to eighty-five cents a can. We buy cases of paint at a New Mexico Pay N' Pak and double up on supplies like masking tape, reams of paper, stencils, pens; the absolute basics that keep us going.

Were Eve to stray, it would not be the snake that tempts her but rather Fred. His charisma cannot be denied. His presence is a crucial force in our work. I don't know who's cooler, Lightning or Fred, but it's definitely a two-way race for the leading man in our daily drama. Lightning is an absolute shredder on the guitar. He and Gilles play down the moon almost every night, a guitar duo of unmistakable magics.

Beyond all this, Dawn and I have entered our own new phase. Maybe it's me starting to seriously consider the future for the first time in months. Maybe it's the road. I imagine the history of cinema through another lens: everyone fucking everyone. Directors and actors, writers and script girls, all the people that make magic happen, sleeping together and trying to keep it quiet; how many make it through? We're about to enter a phase called production, and I carefully consider the parallels between our story, the real story, what I want it to be, and the false narrative that only exists in my head.

We spend a morning alone together, scouting the rising construction sites of new neighborhoods in East San Antonio, taking notes for Eve's map to help fill in the future, something seen more clearly out here on suburban streets. The cul de sacs that will soon enclose the bloodlines, making a safe life for hundreds of new families. We watch workers like ants swarm the streets as we drive around, striving to finish their jobs, only to quickly start the next. The American nuclear family is never so clear as when you get to observe the foundations laid out in all their preplanned, ordained organization before the humans move in. I can see it all, far into the distant future. Larger, connecting streets with stoplights at the edge to escort you to your job and back again in a safe, orderly fashion. Little parks scattered throughout the middle, modern slides and lots of bark so no one gets hurt. Place the new school across the street from the mini mall so the kids have somewhere to put into action everything they've been taught. It all seems so ideal; how could it possibly fail? It's a perfect time to check in with her.

"Would you ever live in a place like this?"

She shakes her head, taking it all in as I'm doing.

"Doubt it. But who knows? Being young precludes one from serious consideration of such matters."

"Yeah, well, people our age do buy houses, you know. I bet they don't feel precluded." She laughs.

"They probably don't. But people like us, we're cut from a different cloth, aren't we?"

She reaches over and strokes my arm, a gesture that feels as if she's simply trying to get me to comply, to obey. It's the sublime, don't go there technique. Screw that.

"I could live in a place like this. There's something to be said for stability and safety."

"You think?"

"I think it's presumptuous to assume stability defers creativity or freedom, which is what I think you think."

"Maybe."

"I think there's freedom to be had here, even in a single playground, or a quiet bedroom. All of these can bring great freedom, if one knows how to look, how to see."

"And how would you pay for all this freedom?"

I stop the van at the corner, seeing what she sees.

It's a family, at the site of their new home, standing next to a new car. Father, mother, small child and another on the way, obviously moving into the structure that nears completion. They are talking to a contractor of some kind, and everyone seems happy and excited. Dawn coughs out a mocking laugh.

"God, if that ever happens to me, shoot me."

Seeing something completely different and obviously disgusting to her, and with nothing further to say, I take my foot off the brake and turn to exit to the neighborhood. I suppose I should be happy. Instead, for the moment, I feel lost, with no clear sight back, or forward.

The one who Shanghaied me is the one I have trusted the most. Are her motives questionable and from time to time downright harsh? Her intent is not always known to me, and occasional skepticisms about her motives leech into my brain. I find myself attached to her in a way that defies outside influence and while wild and consensual, is not healthy. We are a team, but my willingness to do what she wants when she wants it is a constant reminder of how weak-willed I am, not just with her but in general. I catch myself deferring to her in a way that is unsound, not unlike a stray dog she picked up.

We're the painting team that gets the best returns and the best tips, however, which we hide in her boot. I want to hide a few bucks in my shoes too, I protest, but she laughs and kisses me, and, like a fool, I don't. Also like a fool, I let it drop and don't bring it up again, being merely grateful for this experience that she's brought me into. We save it for spending money elsewhere down the road. When no one's looking, I stuff a ten-dollar bill into my pocket, eager to build an argument.

I'm constantly stealing the words out of her mouth for my script, a theft of her alliterative style of speaking in overly dramatic, nonsensical accents. Example: In a high, twee British accent one day, out of nowhere, she sings:

"The way the day is made, she said, she said in ways that made her head, into a way that led her to, investigate the thoughts ahead," laughing to herself.

She quickly shifts into false, Python-esque brogue.

"Ya'kay in me book, lad. Pure drish must daze, boot tuday ya fine, boy," as she pulls me to her and kisses me on me cheek.

Southern accents, surfer tongues, and Gothic cadences, all high drama and endlessly entertaining. I type what I can, the results looking like nonsensical beat poetry, but also realizing it might be a code or map to something, something bigger than words. Are monsters really controlled by spells? The way she speaks, the lilts that make one laugh or simply join in as she sings and whistles through the days are easily adaptable to the page. I find inspiration in it, every day a musical library of ideas. My writing is benefitting from this relationship, although I'm embarrassed to admit that the advantage which she derives from our agreement is, admittedly, more physical than I'm comfortable with. I get the sense that without our physical connection she just might undermine me or simply not be as supportive as she would be if we weren't fucking all the time. It gets old. Too much of anything, sex included, is overrated.

I've written two strong acts, and Dawn is crucial in the creation. She takes ideas and thoughts and reorganizes them in ways that, when she leans in close to whisper them to me as I clack-clack-clack on the crappy old Smith-Corona I picked up for five bucks at a thrift store, I type what she says and it comes out great, almost every time. Dialogue and scene descriptions that seem to flow out of us like some dark, mysterious machine. The story of our film is still secret, no one knows what brews in our private talks. If anyone asks, I show them my notes of her talking and I get a weird look. The best poetry always hides in plain sight, safe from suspicion.

Maybe that's all this is, some scrawled ideas and high-spirited conversations, never to amount to anything. The fear of any young artist, or of anyone for any reason at all—is to have it all come to naught. I can't let that fear enter though. The monster that lingers at the back of my mind has, to this point in my life, been kept on a leash, an invisible choker of indecision that keeps it at bay, under control. A monster I keep around for inspiration, but good God what if it got loose? At the picnic table I type by flashlight late into the night until a voice from the darkened bus calls for me to quit.

"Dude, that typewriter. Shut the fuck up!"

I glance at her one day while we're in some gigantic thrift store in some forgotten dusty town and observe quietly, seeing her as strangers see her. Tall, lean and stark, a sternness that easily turns to a bright star full of magic. She's the rebirth of someone, or something, I think. Her crazily cropped couture, self-styled on a whim one afternoon after scoring a vintage clipper set and a box of thrown-out hair dyes from a dumpster, is half Siouxsie Sioux and half Jean Seberg. Her intensity is Frida Kahlo-esque with a dash of Charlie Chaplin for the kids.

She sees through you, a storyteller looking for secret angles and private parkways to wander into. How I was so quickly sucked into her gravitational pull is clearer now. Licking her hand that first night, telling her there weren't enough scoundrels in her life, being high on drugs were all universal, a warning beacon fired off from the end of an era being abandoned to us, both looking for something new, something less passive.

Men and women alike are drawn to her magic, either lusting after her unique bone structure or curious about the strange energy in their midst, subconsciously wanting to be something like her.

We make eye contact across the store and begin to entertain each other, silently, like an old nitrate film, wandering through others personal histories. Holding up items to show one another across the room, we take turns trying to make the other laugh without speaking.

Little gestures like slipping on an old dusty bowler hat, sipping from a cracked coffee mug that says 'No. 1 Dad' or lifting weights quickly evolves into dirtier territory. I mime a broom handle being used for posterior purposes, she walks up behind a stranger and without him seeing makes ridiculous faces behind his back until he turns, her face immediately returning to normal, nothing wrong here. The man looks at me.

Ed walks over and asks me a question, and by the time I look back to continue the game, she's already moved on. I watch her as she browses the used books and videotapes, unaware she's still being observed and yet still almost acting. Sweeping gestures as she holds up items to inspect, like she knows the secret—her life is the play she's the star of. I'm used to staring at her, but here in this worn-out old store on this dusty old continent the adoration I have starts to vibrate in me, and I feel charged with something, not just the film but all of it, not just for her but for this whole thing. It rings in me, and I have to step outside.

On a call back home, I tell my mother she's someone I can't figure out. It may be love, but I still firmly believe that there are better things than that. On today's call, Mom is unaware that, currently, Ed has talked me into getting naked in the phone booth, standing alone in the middle of nowhere, for a photo shoot on his old janky polaroid camera. I'm posing nude as I'm talking to her. Everyone comes out of the bus to laugh at his little photo shoot.

"What's all that laughing I hear?" Goodnight, Mother.

Dawn and I spend a lot of time together naked, for that matter the whole family is stripped down as much as possible. Being nude has its own set of rules and guidelines. We can't just prance around in our birthday suits anywhere. We're still in America and, as Heather and Gilles will attest, most folks don't have the stomach for real freedom, neither in active participation nor mere observance, regardless of how beautiful we all truly are. Freedom in America seems more and more like an idea people cling to and love to broadcast and talk about but never really participate in. In towns and cities, we keep the clothes on. But once we're out, our crew is a bunch of beautiful bodies, letting it all hang out. It's liberating. It's human.

Heading back to civilization, the costumes joylessly come back on, readying ourselves for the next act, this play we've all been cast in. Places, everyone. And then, fully clothed on a Monday morning, we're back to work. Hip pockets stuffed with maps and stacks of fliers in hand, the teams arise as we come to a stop at the edge of suburbia.

We never drive the bus into a neighborhood, it's a choice Adam made years ago to avoid as much suspicion as possible. From the driver's seat, in his recently scored German Chancellor helmet and wraparound shades, he dramatically cranks open the bus door to a blaring cassette of John Philip Souza marches. We all salute as we march down the steps, stoned, into the neighborhoods of destiny, our part in this great drama unfolding as we share our message of safety, of address numbers.

"Paint, paint, paint, you sons of bitches," is his jovial send off, our marching orders as we're dropped every morning at various points across ever-growing neighborhoods full of friendly homeowners who are always ready with a fun comment or a cold soda.

How truly glorious it feels, how charged and alive, to be in a place so unknown, doing a job that no one has any knowledge of, making more than most college graduates and in a time when everything seemed so new. The nineties are full of hope and promise, and here we are, right at the outset, thriving in secret on the backs of the capitalist pigs, but on our own terms, not theirs. To the government, we give nothing back. To the people, we deliver as much love and kindness as we possibly can in the short spurts of time within which we connect to them.

A curb paint job, one house, typically lasts no longer than ten minutes. In that span of time, we greet passerby, smile and thank the residents and share our tales as quickly and clearly as we can.

You want to learn how to pitch something effectively? Start with one minute to pitch and an eight dollar ask. It's great practice for the future to come.

12

IT'S NOT THAT I MIND teaching people how to ride a skateboard. It's the fact that it's actually difficult and depending on your sense of balance and dexterity, for most people it's hard to pick up. The time it takes, the physical effort you must invest, you have to be a glutton for pain and humiliation.

The weeks, the months—thousands upon thousands of hours spent learning how to ride up a pool wall, then kick turn and come down again? Years. The last thing we want out here is a broken wrist or arm, the two likeliest contenders in the "let's learn how to ride a skateboard" debate with amateurs whose confidence always goes from one hundred to zero the first time they fall and slam into unforgiving concrete. It really, really hurts.

And so, here we are in East Texas at an amazing find: massive, fifty-foot concrete pipes. Massive, smooth and clean, abandoned in the middle of nowhere, a place we always try to camp. Wherever we go, we always call camp 'nowhere.' That way, we never lie to anyone when they ask us where we live.

"So, where you folks staying?"

"Nowhere."

We find this place like we do so many other awesome, secret sites; accidentally, brought on by a desire to remain anonymous and live off the land for free, somewhere outside the sight of prying eyes.

They're huge, clearly for some massive but currently sidelined water project as they seem to have been here for a while. The number-one rule of skateboarding: waste no time. As soon as I see them, I've grabbed my board and I'm out of the bus, immediately pumping back and forth getting higher and higher, the family comes out to watch.

Adam, of course, wants to try. Anything that is remotely cool or wild, Adam's gotta try it. Just last week, he hopped a fence and rode a wild donkey we spotted in an open field, much to the delight of everyone assembled. He got tossed after a few seconds, but he did it. He's that guy.

No harm, no foul.

"Have you ever ridden a skateboard?" I ask, tightening my belt as far as it will go so my pants won't sag. These past few months have left me leaner than I've been since I was a kid.

"Not in a long time, but it looks pretty easy."

Yeah, easy.

You ever heard the saying "an artist makes hard work look easy?" The art you see on a gallery wall, the piece that makes you think, I could do that.? That is the talent of all artists regardless of their medium, to make hard things look simple.

I've been riding since 1978, twelve-plus years of practice, practice, practice. I'm no hack, and I can definitely ride these pipes. But I've never looked up at a concrete pipe the size of a house out of the blue and say, "I bet I could skate that."

The course of fate dictates that, of course, Adam nails it. And while it can be annoying to see someone succeed so quickly at something I've tried my whole life to be good at, it makes sense. He's got the build of an athlete but the moves of a dancer. He's the random chance, the one-in-a-hundred outlier that watches someone do something for a few minutes, tries a couple times and wipes out hard.

"I got it," he says, shaking it off.

He doesn't get very high in the pipe, but he can ride it, back and forth, kick turns that are wild and loose, surfing the barrel in a sloppy, dangerous way, both hands always in that ridiculous "hang loose" sign, his sandblasted curly black hair jutting out from under his thrift store score, an old German helmet. Everyone cheers—he loves people watching him perform. With only one skateboard, my cherished Mark Gonzalez street model, Adam and I take turns riding this monster as the sun sets. Eden sits on the board, all of us taking turns pushing her up and down the transitions as she laughs and laughs. Eventually, after a round of dumpster-score dinner (canned beef, potatoes, and soda) everyone else retires to the bus and vans for sleep.

Adam and I build a small fire near the edge and try to go higher, higher. I finally wipe out, after making it past vertical a couple times, eventually shooting my board into the stars, too tired to try again. That night we sleep there, in the bottom of the pipe in crusty, Vietnam-era sleeping bags with gigantic throw pillows.

Adam is full of questions about the history of skateboarding, so I tell him stories about Alva, Hawk and Hosoi, the Gods of flight, of power, until he falls asleep. I watch the stars move across the pipeline, fading into infinity. Today, I was the teacher.

MONSTERS

13

SITTING AROUND the campfire one night, I blurt out our film idea to the family. "We should make a monster movie."

On a whim, and without consulting Dawn, I tell everyone of our monster movie script and our hopes to shoot a film with them all. A few months ago, I wouldn't have dared to make such a move without consulting her first, but our private conversations are like small military camps, moving ever closer to the battlefield that is film production, and I feel more confident than ever that our plans and strategies will be widely accepted. It's the first time I ever pitch a movie in my life, and the wine and weed have emboldened me. Adam, sensing economic danger and perhaps a shift in the power dynamic, immediately jumps in as the foil; his unhinged, stereotyped version of what he thinks a Hollywood producer sounds like.

"No, no, no! It's all wrong!", he says, in a voice that makes kids laugh and adults smile. "Youse gotta find a better love interest here, that what ya need. More blood. More blood! Shockers! I need scare tactics and love scenes, forget all that art/life stuff. I need to put asses into seats, kid."

I get the feeling he senses instinctively what real film producers say. Getting defensive, I remind him that the monster, in its way, *is* the love interest, however hideous and maligned, and there's no way to change that. Two can play the drama game.

"I'm a writer, damnit, not an ass-kisser!" Everyone laughs.

The fire blazes as a sliver moon climbs over our ragged desert campsite. Adam and I go full Barton Fink on our performance routine, laughing at ourselves as the characters we're now performing—writer vs. producer—become more insane, more bellicose. Joints get passed around with the last of the wine, and we're all now in full madcap theater mode. Everyone's high, and some mushrooms we scored a few days back don't last the night. The bonfire rages, everyone's faces lit up by the wooden pallets we grabbed in town, and ten feet away, total darkness. The contrast between light and dark is buzzing in my mind, I see it all as a shot from another unknown film, a test reel of my resolve, my determination to see this through. Every one of us is an ancient mask, all participating in the ritual of the moment, hanging on words, a steady diet of fire and void.

I've had few opportunities in my life to launch into a routine so focused and bizarre, so loaded with bizarre byzantine detail and hopped-up hilarity, yet so profound as that night with Adam. This madness is fireside improv, and I boldly stride into new waters with no concern for the straight world a million miles away. Thirty minutes of this banter go by.

"Where we gonna get that much blood?" he asks after I explain a particularly harrowing murder scene. I turn to Lightning, who I've already spoken to in confidence about such things.

"Yeah, I can make awesome blood packs. Karo syrup and food color. Easy."

"You? You *knew* about this?" Adam feigns shock at Lightning's knowledge, to which we all laugh. I parry and strike at his every move to stop this idea of making a movie. I seem to be losing ground. Dawn rises to her feet.

"I'll direct. It's both our idea, but let's be honest: I'd be the best director, right?"

Everyone claps as she goes around the circle giving high fives. She stops and faces the group, serious now, almost empty bottle of wine in hand, letting the circle cast her at center stage, her silver necklaces shimmering in firelight, eyes lit up by the moon.

"There's no reason *not* to do this. We are a well-oiled machine, ready for more action. I say more power to the people!" Again with the clapping and hooting. She smiles at Adam, who sees what she's doing, turning the team, probably for the first time ever. It's a brilliant, calculated move, because it's not stopping the workflow. He retains all power, we're just asking for permission to do an art project, and there's going to be a need for a budget, however small. Dawn and I have already discussed this in private, we don't mention it now, but we believe we can make it for a thousand bucks. It's simply adding another element of crazy to a world that's already insane. His look mirrors what we all feel: we all love her so much. We continue, high drama arguments and ridiculous humor, thrusting and making theater for the evening's entertainment. Adam goes to the questions phase, a good sign that a pitch is about to close, and a deal is about to be made.

"What about locations?" Dawn gestures to the moonlit landscape.
"Set in the desert."
"What about actors?"
I make a sweeping motion of everyone assembled.
Eden even gets in on it. "I want to be an actor, Daddy."
Everyone nods in agreement.
"Call me Howard," Adam says in his "money bags movie guy" voice.

At his every statement, we lash back with artistic plight and plea for some form of creative control over this project. It's now turned from antic theater to a real idea. Yes, we can actually shoot a film, here, in the desert. It's not impossible. We've made it clear that in fact, it's more possible here than anywhere else in the universe. We've got the writer, cast and crew, and more importantly (never mention the money), we've got the passion. He's back on his heels now, but Dawn decides not to knock him down. Not yet.

"None of us would be here without you and this magical life you've created, that is one hundred percent true. We are all so grateful." Everyone nods in agreement as she steps around the fire to him and kisses his forehead. Everyone goes quiet. His eyes narrow, he's on the verge of either acquiescing or denying. Then, out of nowhere, he pulls a cigar, *a fucking cigar*, out of his pocket, chews on it reflectively, his Hollywood mogul brain working on the information laid out before him. A fucking prop. Goddamn, this guy's good.

Dawn laughs, knowing when someone has a higher card. He lets the tension build as everyone awaits his reply. Dawn and I sit, eager to be seen as obedient and willing to accept his decision. It's the end of the show, this is real now, everyone can sense it. He glances around the circle, looking deeply into each one of us.

It's weird; I sense from him a love so intense and profound that it's not dissimilar to what I imagine watching a child be born is like, if your child was a no budget horror movie. And then, with all the authority of his position as captain of our itinerant band of painters and travelers, he lights the cigar, gets a big puff up, walks over and pats Dawn and I on our cheeks.

"Good pitch, kids. Looks like you got yourselves a movie."

Everyone claps. In a last flourish, I take a knee and kiss the moonstone ring on Adam's pinky, a gesture of fealty to which everyone heckles me.

Dawn hugs him. Everyone hugs because they can feel it -they know they've all just been given the permission to get even crazier. Beers kept cold in the bus are broken out, a couple only, but shared around, a taste is all you need to bind the moment. The vibe is real. This was one of the many ways in which we kept our bonds strong. We hug all the time. Many people in the straight world write off hugging but in our world the hug seals the deal. No handshakes, no notes or signatures—the hug signifies validity and faith in one's moral fiber, warranted or not. It's pure. I'm a hugger, like my mother before me.

"Really?" I ask Adam, everyone talking excitedly as the beer bottles make the rounds, "are we going to do this?"

"Fuck it, what else are we going to do? Let's make a monster movie" he says, returning to his West Texas drawl. I don't have the power to believe it until I look at everyone's faces. Dawn shoots me a *good move, babe* look, a wink and a finger down the face that says I brought the tears of joy. It's clear she's proud of my unilateral move. Everyone has that look, we just invested in them too, and the love here is deep. Like church, it's real.

Gilles grabs his guitar, lights a smoke.

"Monster music, minor keys," he says, whipping out an ominous minor chord riff on his guitar while Ed has already started sketching storyboards. Less than two minutes into the deal, we have musicians and artists working on the film, immediately gone to work. I'm high on the idea, so much more than the mushrooms and weed. Drugs don't feel like this. Nothing does. My brain works overtime, its wheels spinning at a furious rate. Eve rises to put Eden to bed, we say our good nights, the show's over.

Gilles and Heather follow to dreamtime as Fred and Morgan decide to go for a late-night walk. Everyone is fading, Lightning and Ed retire to the van as well. Dawn, Adam, and I stay at the fire, drinking and smoking. Adam now speaks in a different tone, to the order of hierarchy: Him, producer, Me, writer, Dawn, Director. I think he realizes he's made for this, making movies. I can see him chewing on it, his dark, blazing eyes cast a glance at the moon, the stars, this place. A long stare at me and Dawn. He can see it clearly too. Probably a totally different vision of the finished product and result, but he's in.

After a long chat about the nature of film production—we're guessing now, as none of us have very clear ideas about how to actually produce a movie—Dawn seems to inherently glean from the ether the math of such things, and Adam falls into character one last time as he heads for his old canvas, WWII-era tent full of sleeping family.

"That script ain't gonna write itself, kid," he turns and says to me. "Finish that thing. I want it on my desk first thing Monday morning. And by desk, I mean that picnic table over there. We start pre-production in New Orleans on the 15th."

He salutes and disappears into the folds of his fabric domicile with a dramatic flourish. Dawn and I share a surprised look. *New Orleans?*

From the tent, Adam the mind reader responds. "Yeah, New Orleans. Pack some clean underwear."

14

AS WE WALK the streets pasting flyer after flyer, day after day, I think about all of it. We need cameras, lights, makeup and blood. Microphones are more important than a camera. Blood, how do you even make real looking blood? Monster magazine memories from childhood flood my daydreaming. We'll need buckets of it. How do you light interiors? Do we need real actors, or can we truly cast from within? We need more weed, but mushrooms are going to have to sit this one out, being difficult to find as it is. This is an eight-dollar-a-day shoot. We make an oath to never pull a single permit on this film, totally underground and illegal. Ed wants to know if he can start constructing giant monster puppet heads. Dawn puts her arm round him.

"Sketches first, babe." She tells him she'll need to approve the art. Adam chimes in.

"There's a guy in I know in Austin that owns a bar, he's trying to start a film festival, I heard." Can we get blood recipes *and* weed from him? We'd be first in line to submit. We need everything, and we need to keep painting, but most importantly, we need a good story.

The best part about writing a script is finishing that first draft. There's nothing more exciting than looking at a story from front to back. Sure, it sucks, and there's plenty that will change and get cut or added, but when it's done, especially laid out act by act on a picnic table, the satisfaction is overwhelming. Everyone was gone curb painting for the day, but with Adam's commitment to the project true, I must double down and stop drifting and dreaming. I need to type the whole thing, and the mere thought makes my hands hurt. With Adam cracking the whip, rewriting eighty pages takes less time than I imagine. I'm required to use the format he pulls from an old theater book he finds at the Gallup public library, and after eight hours I take a long pause as the sun goes down, dust clouds in the distance announcing the arrival of painters, ready to party after they've worked all day.

I've sat at this ancient picnic table for most of the last three days in the blazing sun and simply typed out how this film will work, how I want it to look, to feel, to be understood. I'm organizing in my mind the ideas and impressions and I wonder: *is this what writers do?* Do they spend endless afternoons watching the desert change color and ponder for hours the importance of catching a mere two-second glimpse of a coyote popping his head up at you over a ridge and then away again? I can't help but believe that yes, that is what they do. What *we* do. If I'm a writer then I have done what I believe is right, I've sat and contemplated, letting my thoughts wander and my ideas grow, scribbling notes that I've pounded into a script that we'll hopefully turn into a real horror show.

Film Synopsis-working title **'Demons From Beyond'**

When an overzealous real estate developer, looking to build an exclusive gated community in the desert outside of Phoenix is warned of an Indian curse, he disregards it. As construction moves forward, horrible things begin to happen to all involved in the development.

Simultaneously, a group of hippie kids heading west across Arizona in a giant school bus meet a Native shaman who warns them of same, but they take it seriously, especially after a member of their group drinks tainted ground water and falls mysteriously ill. The lad disappears on the full moon and is transformed by Native sorcery and mercury poisoned water into a hideous, half man, half beast with a misshapen form and long, dagger-like teeth that jut out of his mouth at impossible angles, a primordial hellhound. The mercury leeched into the ground water from the government's long-abandoned underground nuclear tests. Here, members of tribes who once lived in harmony lash out against each other in the aftermath of a full solar eclipse many years ago. The madness has returned. The cursed, infected boy becomes a hideous, murdering creature: The Amarok — part wolf, part man, and all vengeance.

The Amarok wreaks havoc by killing construction workers, a rancher, a golfer, etc. He menaces the neighboring communities. In the end, the development is shelved, abandoned to rot in the desert, solving the killings is more than the government can handle. Some places were meant to be left alone.

I admit: the story is derivative. I've brazenly lifted ideas and elements from several lesser-known films, like John Frankenheimer's *Prophecy* and John McTiernan's *Nomads*, but in the end, I've made it my own and learn, years later, that this approach is not only accepted but encouraged when one is starting out. A story costs nothing to create, just time and dedication, a commitment to sit down and do the work. A film is all money.

Adam holds all the cash collected from curb painting at all times, except for the pocket money we're all allowed, and of course whatever we can squirrel away here or there, never more than fifty or sixty bucks. He commits to buying a camera and sound gear before we leave for New Orleans and by that time, we'll need a finished script. With a barely existent budget we cannot afford missteps or mistakes. We need structure. Adding and subtracting ideas, characters, even whole plotlines as the project shoots would be disastrous, and the amounts of ideas thrown at me from everyone over the last two days alone has me nervous and overwhelmed. Lightning wanders over, his pitch firmly in mind.

"How about we set part of it in space?" How about no. Heather stops by my office later in her newly buzzed pink mohawk, giving me her two cents on which direction to go.

"Can there be a musical number? Like, punk style?" Dance choreography, no way. I wish. Even Ed wanders in to get some ideas off his chest.

"How hard is it to blow up a car? I know a guy..." I have to put my foot down.

"No explosions. These are all crazy ideas that have nothing to do with our pitch: a monster movie, remember? I'm concerned we're all smoking too much or too little dope." Everyone seems to bristle at my accusations, but Dawn nods in agreement.

"It's true. The way we live is counterproductive to what a film shoot should be: organized, well planned, and consistent. If we can paint two hundred curbs in a day, we can do this. We can do both, but there needs to be consistency." Even Fred doubles down as an immediate supporter of the film.

"This isn't some silly monster movie, guys. This is real," making the plea. He continues.

"We can create catharsis by making an artistic representation of horror by playing at it and divining meaning through shock and terror, thereby also purging our own darker emotions."

Everyone seems to be okay with Fred's stoned assessment. I agree. And yet, I'm afraid I'm not good enough and it'll all fall apart. Fear fills my heart: *it will be my fault.* Somewhere down deep, the beast that is fear tries to tell me I am none of these things. Yet, we're buying equipment in three days and leaving in a week. Dawn shrugs off my concern.

"Relax. We've got this. Everyone is behind us, even Adam." She's a shaft of light in the world of writing; of things misshapen and misunderstood, where vengeance and revenge have legitimate claims on this world and cannot be stopped by the laws or weapons of man. The blood of my monster has begun to flow into our lives. When I look back, will I be able to say I did the best I could? I can't tell. I do know I've never pushed so hard for something in my life, and there's no way I'm turning back.

This will end in the completion of a movie, a nameless thing constructed in a world no one knows. On the road. No money, no rules. A cockeyed, half-baked experiment that is now being brought to life, in a landscape that seems perfect for the resurrection of vengeful things and violent, if well-meaning, deities. Upon Adam's approval of the film, I immediately start sleeping poorly. In the great outdoors, don't let your imagination get the better of you. Don't take too much and let it get under your skin and freak you out.

In the desert, you can't sleep with the lights on.

We blow through almost five hundred bucks, which seems to be a lot of money to me, but Adam doesn't seem concerned. He decides we're shooting our film on a Sony Video 8, one of the first 8mm camcorders. He buys all the tapes they have in stock—fifteen. I convince him to buy a 16mm camera as well, an old Vitascope hand crank for a cool forty bucks because I knew that real movies are shot on film, not video. The salesman at Dante's Cameras in Farmington tries to hook us up with a crazy Russian 16mm with five lenses and battery packs and chargers that could be modified to charge off your car battery, but we pass. Video is what the boss says, so video it is.

I test the Vitascope. It works. We grab a few small reels of B&W 16mm stock and a change bag after a ten-minute course from the kid behind the counter on how to load film in the bag—eternally valuable. We load up on sound gear, a boom pole, cheap-o lights for interior shots, and cases to carry everything in.

We pound a couple beers in the parking lot to celebrate the equipment purchase, then grab lunch and share script notes at a Jack in the Box, reveling in the excitement that always comes before starting a new project.

Fun fact: the cases for the mics were stenciled "Satan's Stallions," a band name I've never found a mention of anywhere, at any time. The Internet is a clearing house tool, and it sweeps almost all information into itself today, so it's a damn pleasure when I seriously search for names like Satan's Stallions and nothing comes up, ever. Multiple searches over decades. Things that started and ended before the internet have the greatest chance of escaping, making it to truly hidden and obscure status. Were they kids who were better at painting cases than playing music? Never made a single recording? In the bygone days of pre-Internet, a lot slipped away. I love that. Rest in Peace, Satan's Stallions, wherever you are.

15

FOURTH OF JULY, Farmington, New Mexico. The Southwest is the best of all things America on Independence Day, parades full of farm equipment and FFA groups, cheering families of cowboys and Indians. Stained, gap-toothed old timers and gleaming Mormon children, all drunk or high on candy before noon. Everyone's all smiles and jokes, on display for the whole county to see. Fireworks of only the most dangerous nature. We get most of our curb painting done the day before, so Adam encourages us all to take in the holiday and have a little fun. We splinter into groups and hit the town. Adam and Eve disappear with Eden to the rides at the fairground.

The rodeo is packed. We hear from Fred that over at the fairgrounds speedway, Lightning has grabbed a position as the driver for one of the local wrecking yards' entry into the high-stakes demolition derby. I never got the opportunity to drive a car for my father's wrecking yard, but I've been to a derby or two, so I knew what to expect. The drivers in these things were often just the parts pullers from the local yards, guys who can strip a car down to its purest form in an hour. Guys who know how to pull a stereo or remove a third member in seconds flat. A cool two hundred dollars will go to the man who can unleash the most destruction.

Guys like Lightning (attractive, well-built gearheads that have a name you want to scream across the speedway) are coveted in the demolition circuit. The drivers' fearlessness and radical approaches to avoiding destruction are what packs the bleachers. Trying to avoid crashing your vehicle into others is easy; attempting to destroy all other vehicles in your path is an art not many master. Dawn, Ed and I grab tickets and get seats on the wooden bleachers, way down front. Within minutes, Dawn has created a cheering section.

"Light-ning, Light-ning," we all drunkenly cheer. Fred and Morgan show up; like the rest of the crowd, they're tipsy on their way to drunk. Fred has won one of those giant plastic megaphones from the milk jug ball games and he screams into it across the track.

"Drive, drive, drive you bastards!" Everyone in the stands laugh. Kids are swirling cotton candy on their arms and getting loaded on sugar and second-hand smoke, adults are pounding the cheapest, coldest beer known to man. It's a sweltering ninety degrees by eleven, probably going to hit a hundred by noon. From the stands we spot Lightning. He does an air guitar riff then waves to the crowd, impeccably dressed in an old, cracked San Francisco Forty-Niners helmet and cutoffs, with a pink T-shirt that says, "Save a tree, eat a beaver." He's so fucking cool and attractive, in that way that all men love and respect in other men who are simply better than them in the realest of ways: he is kind, muscular and tanned, well-read and prolific at almost everything; on this particular day he's a trifecta of cool: poet, guitar shredder, and demolition driver. We love our Lightning God.

The competition looks stiff. While he's got a great ride, a '66 Cadillac with old tires bolted to the sides and front to avoid getting crunched and taken out, there's also a Chrysler Imperial and an early seventies Caddy that look formidable, plus a host of other late sixties sedans and wagons, all with a variety of advantages and disadvantages. Exhaust pipes are channeled up through the roofs of some cars that make them appear more like mechanical dragons and demon steeds, belching filthy black exhaust, ready to launch into the breach. As they all do their parade lap around the track, a cloud of planet-destroying filth chokes the bleachers and the crowd roars its approval. The thunder as they enter the arena is deafening. This fight is to the finish, it's going to be epic, and the multitude gathered here have roared their approval.

Driving backwards is key to winning a demolition derby, for one simple reason: the radiator is in the front of all cars. You lose your water; you lose your cool. Game over. It becomes obvious very quickly that the common strategy to domination is rear-ending the front of other cars, which everyone is trying to do all at once in a mud choked palace of disaster.

The roar of the vehicles keeps the crowd fired up and very quickly one, two, three cars are out. Spectators throw beer cans at cars with regularity, and no one disapproves. If you need to know which American holiday allows and even encourages you to throw your beer cans at cars, drive drunk, and no one bats an eye, the Fourth of July is it. A tow truck drags the losers away while the remaining competitors sit on the sidelines, idling and waiting to launch into battle once more.

A woman in a pink halter top and cutoffs approaches Lightning during a halt and dumps a beer into his mouth, spilling it everywhere. He's a madman. The tow truck pulls out the victims of destruction and soon it's down to Lightning and the Imperial. While he's battered and smashed beyond belief, somehow, in a stroke of genius, Lightning gets his apponent up onto the concrete barrier that surrounds the arena. Wheels off the ground, the Imperial has nothing to do; he's stuck, and that's enough for the judges to call it: Winner by unanimous decision, it's Van's Auto Wrecking and their Caddy with Lightning at the wheel. The crowd roars its approval as he pulls up to the bandstand, climbs onto the roof of his idling, totally destroyed, but still functioning beast. He removes his helmet, rips off his shirt and throws them both to the women in the crowd, who of course go totally nuts.

His long dark hair blows in the exhaust fumes as he gives the tricky Dick double peace signs. He stands triumphantly on the roof of his destroyed Caddy, a Native American kid celebrating the destruction of the white man's death machine on the Fourth of July. The car suddenly drops into drive and tosses him from the roof. His battered, beaten car lurches forward into several rodeo clowns who are prepping for the barrel ride up next. No clowns are hurt, but in a true sign of the times the entire crowd can't stop laughing, cheering for destruction and decadence in a world gone mad. Happy Birthday, America.

The day passes as we drift through the fairgrounds. We're aware of the fact that the way we dress, which is pretty much like extras from some John Waters film. The way we carry ourselves makes us stand out in the places like Farmington. It tells the locals: you're not from here.

The road scene in the 80s was kind of crazy already, what with serial killers prowling the interstates and weirdo creep cults pulling for new converts from every corner of the country. Police are always on the lookout for kids who often need to do nothing more than call the family back wherever to tell them they're not dead. Today, however, Dawn commits the most dangerous of all road moves: the knife dance.

Her defense is unassailable. Multiple witnesses observed clearly drunken men-one big, one small- harassing us at the Ferris wheel. No stranger to dealing out verbal shutdowns, Dawn is usually dressed in black boots, weird flowing dresses, denim vests with Satanic artwork on them, fucked up weirdo hairstyles that no one else dares, and every shirt she owns bears slogans designed to harass and incite. She gets heckled often; there is no doubt amongst us she likes it. With a crowd once distracted by colored lights and pretzel hustlers, everyone now pauses at the escalating verbal skirmish on the midway to see what'll happen next. When called a lesbian biker by one of the drunks, she merely laughs.

"You'll never be half the man your mother was." The crowd laughs at this zinger, and now feeling the weight of embarrassment, the little guy pulls a knife.

"Alright, bitch, let's see how funny you are now!"

A couple people in the crowd call him out. A Mormon looking guy steps forward, eager to bring the situation down a couple notches.

"Come on man, there's kids here. We're all just having fun. Put the knife away." The drunk's not having it, however.

"I'm going to teach this freak a thing or two, see if I don't!" This guy definitely has little man syndrome.

Dawn shakes her head, more annoyed than anything.

"Come on brother, let's just have a good time. I'm sorry I insulted you. Really. I'm sure you're a model specimen of our species," Dawn says, remaining firmly out of reach but not backing down, either. This guy is furious, and somehow that's amusing to her. I would never stick around in a situation like this, I'd be the guy that runs. She knows she's being crass, but she can't help herself. People laugh at this too. More angered than ever, he moves towards her. Ed and I try to stand up for her, a mistake. She shoves us both away.

"Back off. I got this fool." In an effort to de-escalate, she distracts him by lifting her skirt a bit, a tease, which gets the men in the quickly gathering crowd whistling and on her side. In the momentary confusion, the drunk steps close and tries to actually stab her—this guy is nuts drunk, the kind of guy that wanders into the street and starts swinging at cars—and then viola - she swipes the knife away and trips him. She turns, holds it up to show the rubes, who of course laugh maniacally as the drunk tumbles to the ground. It all happens so fast. The guy is pissed off, but she can't see his anger turning to rage. She is the center of attention now and she loves it. Music from the funhouse is the soundtrack to the scene, multicolored lights from the Ferris wheel cascade over the action.

She's launched into violent street theater; sharp weapons bring out the worst in us all. He's quickly back on his feet, stumbling, but ready for round two. It's gone into crazy West Side Story dance/street fight mode as they circle each other, onlookers heckling the drunk guy, him cursing and her laughing. It's only a second before he moves on her, to which she again easily sidesteps his lunge and stabs him in the side. It's more of a poke, she quickly taps him on the side, you can see there's no way it's fatal, but again—she can't help herself. It's over in a second. The whoosh of silence that immediately follows as everyone realizes they've just witnessed a stabbing and then as quickly as the silence—*pow*—the crowd goes nuts. Everyone's yelling.

I'm watching it all, trying to see a quick exit where of course there is none. I'm freaked out; watching a woman you love stab a drunk maniac in front of a crowd of country folk lit up by carnival lights and seeing people coming out of the haunted house, the fun house and down those crazy slides with the burlap sacks, all looking on with expressions that say *what the hell is going on out here?* is an experience I can't recommend, but it is something else. I think about how we're running out of time.

On a whim, as people run in every direction, I grab her around the waist, eyes meeting, a kiss before the end. The look in her eyes as our tongues meet can only be described as sadness, and I'm freaking out as I realize she's definitely going to jail. She breaks away, smiles and takes a bow and sticks the knife into the earth—a fucking bow, as if it's all a performance—when a security guard, finally arriving too late, tackles her to the ground. Everyone's screaming at everyone else, the anarchy lasts for a moment longer.

"I'm dying" the drunk guy moans, which seems absolutely impossible, but what do I know? Maybe he is dying.

A heart attack or something. Young girls gather to weep over him; he's really putting on a show. People are running everywhere. *This it*, I think, *the goddamn Shakespearean end. We've really done it now.*

Fred and Morgan appear and try to remove Dawn from the scene but it's too late. Police arrive. Flashing cop lights and carnival rides illuminate the surreal scenery. As Dawn is being handcuffed, I see an old farmer in dirty coveralls from earlier at the grandstands just watching, standing there staring at us all, probably the one night a year he leaves the ranch, sucking down a corn dog swathed in chemical yellow mustard in the most unappealing way ever. Then I see Adam too, on his knee in the crowd with the camera rolling. *Holy crap, did he catch all this?* The camera focused on the chaos of cops, people lying, people laughing, sucking down sodas and popcorn. We're defending Dawn, amidst the general madness of it all, and Adam gives me the nod—we're rolling. Cops take us all downtown, just for good measure.

Knife guy was fine, just a flesh wound. Thanks to all the witnesses, there's no way he can press charges on her, or us. We are all let go almost as soon as we arrive at the jail, but Dawn's held overnight. While locked up, she talks to her parents on the phone and gets everything straightened out. When I go to retrieve her the next morning, she's calm and collected.

"I'm sorry I've been so secretive. Watching you talk to your mom on the phone the other day, I realized I need to tell mine about you also. You really mean something to me, you know. I am rather fond of you. You realize you are a fucking weirdo though, right?" She flatters me.

We sit in the jailhouse waiting room, littered with cheap plastic chairs, her finally telling me about her secret life. I'm the first to learn, it seems, that outside of Eve no one knows anything about Dawn.

"I was born in Toronto, but my folks moved to B.C. when I was four. Mum got a gig with old college friends running an experimental theater company that toured the U.S. and Canada." French Canadian. Her parents were once circus performers and now attorneys, both from a small logging town in Ontario, on the shores of Lake Huron. She resents her parents going straight, how they tried to discourage her from a life on the road.

"I hated the fact that they would lament the 'good old days,' yet tell me to avoid a life like the one they lived, as I would inevitably be staring down a long list of financial insecurity and manipulative people." To her, they were hypocrites. Sellouts. "I love them," she says, "but they're old now."

And to her, that was the ultimate crime: not getting old physically, but mentally.

"Everybody ages with time, but we can keep ourselves young and keep passion alive in our hearts if we keep on doing that which we love."

Her parents once touring performers themselves, they knew exactly what it meant when she left boarding school, a prestigious little campus on Seattle's Capitol Hill three years ago. Bored with that scene, one day she just quit, headed south with nothing but a small backpack full of herbal medicines, a giant water bottle, and *The Beast in the Jungle* by Henry James, a novella she tells me is a cautionary tale about not sitting idly by and letting the best years of your life pass. She's been on the road for three whole years. I am humbled, exhausted, and in love with a complex, intelligent woman. I often feel like a rube next to her, although she makes it clear that's not the case.

"You know it's mostly bravado with me, right? You're genuine and sincere, to a fault. I love that about you."

"Well, you did stab a guy at a carnival," I say.

"Yeah, I sure did." We both laugh as we exit the jailhouse.

"Seriously, I have issues and although I love the way in which we live now, please know that this won't last forever. Not this life, out here is…the only constant I want is change…" She seems hesitant to say more.

I lie and tell her I get it, letting the subject change.

"My parents were, are, great models for what I don't want to be, you know?"

I nod, acting like I'm listening but still thinking of the words *this won't last forever.*

She smiles and takes my hand as Gilles pulls up in the van.

We spend the day focusing on rewrites to accommodate our constantly swelling and contracting film budget. The story has been plugging along, and while we still have a lot to achieve, I'm mostly done with the script.

And now, we have this 'filming without a permit' trouble, even though Fred nearly convinced the cops we were just goofing around at the fairgrounds. It's not a huge bust financially, but we're trying to keep as much money as possible in our pockets and our heads down, not exposing ourselves for fines. I'm sure it's because while we all look like freaks, we are also organized and deliberate in our blatant shooting in public. A clapper is a clapper—that's a movie. We're practicing, but we don't act like hobbyists. Boom poles speak to professionalism, no matter the skill level of the operator. It looks like we're doing exactly what we're doing, and there's no attempt to hide it—we're shooting a scene from a film.

There was a time, not so long ago, when you could just go out and shoot scenes in public places, even cities packed with people, cars, kids and glorious backgrounds, and no one would bat an eye. Maybe the occasional glances at the camera from unknowing extras, but usually, even in big cities, you could get away with it. That was a long time ago. Sometimes, here in small-town America, the incidental asshole needs to tip off the authorities to the work of illegal artists, and being the authorities, and usually with nothing more to do than round up dunks, they're compelled to respond. They'd love an excuse to get us out of town, even on a technicality.

All our entanglements with cops over the last forty-eight hours have forced us to reveal everything about our group to the relevant powers that be. All that county fair footage of large groups of people for free, and the great lighting from the Ferris wheel, the knife fight, it's all come to bite us in the ass. We're told not to shoot any more in Farmington until they hear from the New Mexico Film Commission on how to proceed. We're screwed. We apply for a film permit anyway, knowing we can't pay the insurance rider. No longer under the radar, our cover is blown. The police know about our activities already, simply because we pulled another peddler's permit when we started doing business in town. But now they see the film as a source of revenue for the city, and we're forced into arguments among ourselves over where, and when, to shoot. Gilles speaks first.

"This is stupid, we're gonna get in trouble, and for what? Another measly hundred bucks? Let's head south, man!" A long quiet settles around the group. Adam weighs in.

"I don't want to jeopardize what we've created here," he says, standing around the fire that night. "One hundred dollars fills our gas tanks and can feed us for a week. We should disappear for a bit."

He's right. Being invisible to the city while capitalizing on its new developments makes it feel like we're plotting raids into the city to claim our spoils, not a totally inaccurate account. We don't always pull permits, we're often carrying marijuana on us and if one of us gets popped for that, it's curtains. Plus, we're smoking pot almost daily in public restrooms, alleys, and parks while we work away our days. This news does not reach Eve. There is information that should remain concealed; the daily curb painting teams keep their mouths shut.

To risk full censure from the state and lose the ability to paint address numbers in New Mexico would be devastating. The Four Corners area is so profitable right now, if we screw up before cleaning up, the drive to find a new place for an extended period would really suck. Here in the desert, Shiprock towering over all we do, it's clear. We're a little frayed.

Dawn asks, "How long do we need to finish up here, realistically?"

We all look to Adam, but Eve responds.

"If we bust our asses? A month?"

Adam nods in agreement. We've got to finish our work, both curbs and filming, then get the hell out of here. For the moment, it's time to find a new place where we can work unmolested by cops, city officials, and knife-wielding idiots that threaten our survival, not only of this film but of this once-in-a-lifetime opportunity to create, as a family, on our own terms.

Authorities will never cease trying to remind you that in America, as long as you keep your head down, there won't be any problems. Rise up and you'll get it knocked. The State's confidence that they can stop us from making a film simply because of a commission or some law of the land is laughable to us and simply naïve. That's not how we play, New Mexico.

16

TOWN TO TOWN and day by day we lean east, flatter and flatter lands. Into the gutter, again and again. We're in desperate need of cash, and with every passing city we're climbing back up, one curb at a time. San Antonio is a tough town to paint.

Skepticism runs high among new homeowners who are distrustful of outsiders in general, never mind a gang of mixed-race, long-haired freaks from far flung parts of the continent who make their own clothes, walk their own way and wear the greatest thrift store sunglasses known to man. We sing out loud. Boys wearing skirts. Girls wearing homemade overalls and t-shirts that say things like "The Mind Is a Terrible Thing to Taste." Knee-high Doc Martens, Birkenstocks, and bare feet. We may drink beer for breakfast, but we also practice Tai Chi and eat healthy, so it balances out.

We're right here in front of you; take a glance at us in the giant parking lot, over at the edge by the old hippie bus with kids and dogs running around, riding our old beater bikes in circles, laughing. You've seen us. As appearances go, we don't make it easy for ourselves, but who cares? Our curbs are beautiful. The ways and customs of our people are glittering, flashing beacons that say, "this place is cared for." You can't beat a message like that, especially for eight bucks.

We grab our permit but are met with opposition late on a Friday, our last day of painting before we skip the state and head south. It barely registers as a hiccup on the road rules seismograph, but it's worth mentioning: some people are angry about everything, want to stir up trouble wherever they look, and strangely, it often seems they don't even understand why they're mad. It's not just my own observation: capitalism sucks.

When you're able to step outside a system and critique it, some things become glaring. The exploitation required for it to survive and thrive makes a mockery of the system itself, and the human condition, the "live free" notion that so many spout as American flies in the face of the horror show that is an overtly capitalist society.

Economic inequality is never more observable than from the front seat of a rickety old school bus loaded with dropouts from the thrift store generation, wailing on guitars and smoking weed, holding the line in a struggle against the very idea of imperialism and war-based thinking. Our trip is with kindness and love, and music. The trip of capitalism is with power. They want, we are.

This homeowner of opposition thinks he knows everything, and the stuff that evades him is "some bureaucratic horseshit." The problem is he's genuinely unhappy. Like many Americans, he's simply a victim of that most uniquely American of circumstances, being hoodwinked by the capitalist carnival barkers for a new age into a path of mirrors, each more misleading than the last. Arcane mortgage contracts, scurrilous bills that seem to manifest from thin air, a symbiotic servitude that slowly drapes its cloak over him in its attempt to get him to repeatedly consume, consume, consume.

Everything new and wrapped in plastic, processed for the end times; he's been misled, buying a home he can't afford in a place he hates with people he doesn't care about because he's never walked over and just knocked on the next door. And one thing that pisses off unhappy people more than anything is happy people. And here's two of the happiest people he's ever met: Lightning and Ed. Legit happy. Cosmic happy. Curb painter stoned late on a Friday playing a ukulele as they approach his door happy.

Angry Citizen Number One tells them he won't pay the eight bucks and wants the work removed. Instead of letting it go, Ed doubles down and tells him that the flyer was placed in the window by someone in the house which, as the flyer says, gives permission to paint the curb.

Ed's condescending tone infuriates this guy, who goes back into the house, removing the flyer from the window. Returning with cordless phone in hand, he calls the cops.

"I've got some gypsy fags in front of my house (true) and they're demanding money (also true) for some kind of painting scam (false)."

We scam no one. We get our permit like anyone else and carry identification as to such. Ed scrapes the numbers off the curb with his cowboy boot, getting angry himself at this middle-class tool.

When the cops inevitably arrive, Lightning has his photo I.D. but Ed does not. They throw Ed in the cruiser and take him downtown to make sure he's not a runaway or escaped convict. Alas, Ed's an ex-con too. It turns out, a year ago he was released from the clink after time served for the sublime art of deserting his platoon over moral reasons. If you wander the halls of a police station anywhere in 1990, missing persons posters cover the walls. Teenagers, adults, and the elderly too, a mishmash of Americans have either skipped out, walked away or just plain disappeared. Same thing happened with Dawn. Escapism at its finest.

It's a weird time to be an American, living on the edge of two-thousand years of a civilization about to flip the clock and start another millennium. Even here, ten years out, the shift in the way the land lies is palpable. This is not something we're supposed to normalize; we're supposed to be going the other way.

The gang heads to the courthouse to spring Ed, only to find out he has outstanding warrants for unpaid parking tickets from the last several years in California, something the cops in New Mexico failed to catch. Classic. Due to the amount of the fines, he chooses the confines of the Bexar County jail for two days to pay his debt to society for the cardinal sin of not pumping enough dimes into the slot. We tell him we'll be back.

We are thriving on the backs of the subdued, the working class who buy these homes we criticize, yet so desperately need to continue our survival. Without their lifetime investments, we'd be forced to hang it up. It's not lost on us: we need capitalism too. The system itself creates all sorts of ontological ephemera.

Texans will tell us straight to our faces: our appearances are laughable, and they can't believe we do what we do. It's the same everywhere; we're constantly in explanation mode when it comes to the nature of our business and our reality. City officials understand, or at least tolerate us and rarely have questions, but locals by and large seem to get a real kick out of what we're up to. Many are enthusiastic about it and even eager to join up themselves, but when we make the offer to come aboard, the suburbanites don't bite. They like the idea, find it fascinating, but of course they're too busy, too many kids, too much responsibility, too old.

"How the heck would I pay my mortgage?", a common refrain.

We empathize with their plight. Telling them to abandon all that and to bring the kids always brings laughs, as if we all know what no one can really say: you can't break free. Once the system gets its claws in, you may as well call it.

Rare is the individual in a capitalist society who can create their own reality and slip into it. The choices we've made to get us here have surprised and let down many friends and families back home, but we're forging a world of our own on our own terms. And while it's incredibly liberating, it's similarly impossible to explain to someone who's looking forward to buying a jet ski or a new TV. Some like to spend, we like to earn. Everyone gets something out of the American deal.

Two nights later, as we grub around the fire and plan our New Orleans film shoot, a police car rolls into camp. Adam approaches, they speak in hushed tones. After a moment of hushed dialogue, Adam brings the young officer over to repeat what they were talking about.

"Well, your buddy Eddie down there at the jail told me about the movie y'all was makin', and then showed me these pictures."

Silas the cop, a good looking, young rookie and he holds up several oversized pieces of butcher paper with Ed's drawings of our primordial beast the Amarok, as well as some psychedelic storyboards of the main characters. They're passed around. Ed convinced his jailers to not only bring him butcher paper and pencils and let him draw all day, but now he's got a man in the field, bringing his work back home. Panel to panel, Ed sees it all cinematically and nails our story. I'm floored. The artwork is intense. Amarok was making Ed's head spin and it shows in these panels. He's got a real talent, and the cop obviously had an eye for the good stuff.

An art school dropout himself. when asked for a favor by Ed, he complied. Dawn takes the storyboards from Silas and thanks him. She piles on the charm we all recognize as uniquely hers, again pitching the idea to him in her own way.

"Would you consider being in some scenes as a peace officer?" She takes his hand.

"We've got parts for you and your friends if you're interested."

"Sounds great," he says.

She could have been a cult leader the way she drew people in and captured them. And now, we now have the resources of the Bexar County police department. File it under whatever you want, feminine persuasion or movie magic. I'd say he took one look at those drawings and knew we were actually making a real fucking monster movie, and he was in. Everyone wants a piece of that action, especially if there's girls and monsters involved.

17

WHEN I WAS THIRTEEN, my family went to New Orleans on a family trip and I remembered how my mother, nervous in a big, strange place teeming with old-world magic, told my sisters and I to stay close, as kidnappers were everywhere. Here I was, eight years later, an active participant on my own abduction.

Arriving in the Crescent City, we park on the outskirts. We want to drive in, but there's no way in hell we're getting an oversized school bus with a dozen bicycles strapped to the top into the streets of downtown New Orleans. The possibilities for disaster, too great. We pack our bags and hit the street, hop on a city bus, loaded down with mismatched bags and cases of every stripe and persuasion. Guitars, army helmets, large puppets, handmade clothes, colorful humans from every age group, haircuts that reveal our true nature, a madcap cult of trash artists and dropout performers. The passengers of the line 51 bus give us a look of 'just another day' and look away, a refreshing difference from the usual mouth breathing hick who's never seen a real individual. It's a welcome change.

An hour later the bus stops, right in front of Adam's place. A beautiful purple and green sign over the front double doors says 'QED' in the Posada style. He pulls out a key and opens the door. Adam's sister is away, due back in several weeks. The place is ours.

We enter a long, poorly lit hallway with multiple rooms off to both sides. Everyone claims spaces of their own, ending at a spiral staircase. Bags are tossed into rooms as we all run up the stairs, amazed at the layout. The next level is one open space, perfect for dining or dance parties. A long ramp leads from there up to the top floor, a split indoor/outdoor area with showers, stoves, long countertops and a large sink at each end. A giant table commands the glass-enclosed area, the future home of all our monster building, dining and table reads of the script.

We all immediately spread out to enjoy the cosmopolitan city. Amazing cheap food, bars, underground puppet theaters, clowns, and all-night dance parties. Two weeks off curb painting, more than enough time to prep for the shoot and the big curb painting run Adam has planned. Mardi Gras is long past, but this city never seems to sleep or slow down. The signage over the front door we're constantly in and out of, *Quod Erat Demonstratum*, is Latin. Adam claims to have no idea what it means. Fred jumps and slaps it as we pass beneath it:

"That which is to be demonstrated."

The QED is amazing, especially after living in a ramshackle fleet of buses and vans for the last six months. It's a spacious, multi-leveled home that seems more fit for a financially stable family with common sense investments, not a ragtag band of curb painters. Four bedrooms, two bathrooms, and an amazing, oversized patio for giant parties that looks out on the city from the top level. How the hell does a curb painter living in a van own this? Of course, it's not his. Not really. But his reply is as crazy as anything else he says.

"Pop bought it in the late sixties when he won a dangerous bet in Super Bowl IV. Kansas City Chiefs quarterback Len Dawson was his college roommate, and my dad took out a bet that, if he lost, they would have killed him."

Stories like this always poured out of Adam, it's what made his energy so electric.

Rooms claimed, Adam, Dawn and Ed leave with Eden to go grocery shopping, Eve goes to meet with some local friends, and Lightning and I are left on the upstairs patio drinking down the sunset over the gulf, Gilles and Heather close the bedroom door. Fred and Morgan disappear into the dusk.

Later, I disappear into the city alone and find a bar, and myself, at closing time breaking up a fight between an older woman and a young, drunken French cowboy. This is way harder than it may seem, if you've thought of it; that is, breaking up a fight between two very passionate people. I end up spending the night with the couple, learning more about revolution in one night than I thought possible.

The three of us spend the remainder of the evening at the cowboy's apartment, listening to old French revolutionary music records and I am drawn into a revolution of my own, down in the swamp, listening to songs about *Liberte, Egalite, Fraternite, ou la mort.* All Dawn wants to know when I return the next day is if I wore protection. I show her my prize for the evening, a toy gun with the little flag that shoots out the barrel and reads "pow." She laughs and pats the bed next to her. I plead exhaustion.

We pass in the evening or early morning, all either off to bed or just waking up, smiles and quick chats before passing into our new, temporary realities. When I see Dawn walking arm in arm with a strange young man one day, kissing him as he hands her a small book and drops her at the front door, I am filled with jealousy, but only for a moment. I remember my own flight into the arms of strangers only nights before, and I'm reminded we must remain honest and open, and all else will fall into place. Learning to steer clear of petty jealousies and fears is altering my interior landscape, for the better. Still, I need to read. Reading always clears my mind.

I'm at the central library when it opens, eager to walk the aisles. I can spend days in libraries. Growing up in a small town with a great one, I learned the Dewey Decimal system and let it take me to other worlds, other ideas about things unknown and foreign. I settle into an easy chair in the newspaper section and grab a copy of the *San Jose Mercury News.* For just a moment, reading the news of Northern California, I long for home. The reliable repetition, the safety of the same place to lay one's head, the routine stability. The feeling passes. I move on to books, ambling through the stacks and grabbing titles that appeal. New Orleans being a treasure trove of horror, occult, and magic titles, some very old, I make a small pile and escape to the rear of the building, a private little table for the darkness of words. I scribble notes and practice literary thieveries for hours.

Free nights bring free thoughts, and it's a couple days before we even start working on Amarok. When we do, though, the pace is intense. Thanks to Ed's sketches, we're all on the same page. We set up workstations on the upper patio and begin making monster heads and limbs out of a mishmash of scavenged materials. Foam, plastics, chicken wire, and other various ephemera that can hold the form and structure of massive heads and bodies. No sense eating out and wasting our budget, so the BBQ is being run around the clock: breakfast, lunch and dinner.

We decide we're going to operate the monster on a three-wheeled bicycle we score at a thrift store. As we see it, we'll prop the monster up from a frame built to the bike, having one person pedaling, the other puppeteering the legs, giving the illusion of a rambling, club-footed beast of ungodly origin.

Amarok is created in several parts, and we spend days working on latex arms, hands, and legs. Mold work is tough, and many mistakes and failures have led Dawn into a world of surreal, dream-like wolf/elk/bear heads.

There's no denying it: our monster is crazy. Our work would have been truly ridiculous if we hadn't been so sincere. The creation of our beast, the life we gave it, adds an air of dark magic into the reality of our world, the result of a bunch of kids making it up as we went, smoking pot and drinking all day, leaning into the hard reality that we're never going to be like others, so let's just make it our own. A Golem of our own design, the Amarok was something we were truly proud of, born in blood and molded of garbage, cigarettes, sex and love, like us, the castaways of a society in a hurry to abandon the things that bring horror to the doorstep of civilization.

With a mostly finished beast, we practice out front of the QED, pedaling back and forth, in and out of weaving cars, covered in various materials, limping the giant legs and feet out front of the bikes to simulate running. It looks great, if unfinished. After multiple repairs and a few smashed limbs, we get it flowing smoothly. It's actually working—our DIY monster is alive.

Lightning has scored a massive old guitar amp that he plays through on the balcony overhead as we rehearse in the streets, writing our theme song as he watches us pedal around, a dropout dance of death. He strums in a minor key, a doom-like thunder that is ominous enough to get folks passing by on foot to go wide-eyed and panic, if only for a moment. We love to lunge Amarok towards unsuspecting pedestrians who panic and flee, Lightning following our movements in sound, laughter and terror from above. Not just scary monster music, but blues, rock, folk, Americana—he's got a thousand songs memorized.

The best are the songs Gilles and Lightning make up as we go about our days, songs about curb painting, living on the road. Gilles has a hit on his hands, he calls it "Beer Can Trails." It's like living with the musical descendants of outlaw country, thrash metal, and Muddy Waters all rolled into one. They're creating the soundtrack of our lives.

Lightning finds a bar on the main plaza that has great dance nights and we're instantly regulars. Dawn finds a woman across town who teaches her mask making and now she's gone, leaving us to attend to matters of production. When she doesn't return the next day, Adam sees I'm worried.

"She'll be back, don't stress. We lost her for three weeks once." Adam pats me on the shoulder.

I look at him sideways.

"How did she find you?"

"We leave notes at campgrounds, remember? She caught up with us in Durango. Don't worry."

Adam and I are constantly rewriting, playing with cameras, building our own ridiculous version of a Steadicam, experimenting with the particulars. We find a dump with tons of junk plastic and rubber casings from a demolished factory and spend most mornings building and experimenting. Eve and Eden are busy, wandering the city and taking overnight trips to the beach at the tip of a continent that juts into the Gulf of Mexico. Life is busy now, the atmosphere here is conducive to both progress and being laid-back in a way none complain about. Time passes; the script and our monster are ready. We are drinking earlier and earlier every day.

After a week, we shoot our first actual scenes of the film on the streets of New Orleans. No one gives a shit what you do here unless you damage something or someone. We check our footage, which is garbage, and shoot again. Camera and grip lessons are learned and applied. It's looking more and more like not only will this film get made, but that it's going to be amazing. We continue to practice pedaling Amarok with giant poles to elevate and control his various body parts as they are developed and built, then rebuilt to alleviate stress points and make a leaner, crazier and better beast. Thanks to everyone's efforts, we are now making it seem as if the monster is a real thing, running along, a fantastic manipulation that our footage reveals as spectacular and alive. We shoot the monster at sunrise so the light at his back looks magnificent.

Some tough-acting teenage boys come around the corner one day as we're rehearsing and seeing the monster they freak out, grabbing each other and going wide-eyed until they realize it's only a puppet. We roar with laughter. They compliment our Frankensteinian beast, wanting to check out the undercarriage and see how it all works. Rehearsal time is crucial with wonky-ass stuff like this. The puppetry of giant monsters through the streets, the masks, the costumes; everything seems to be arriving at a confluence of clarity that feels rare and of this moment only, in this time and place.

Here we are in the middle of a sprawling American city, prepping a feature film on no money, with no formal knowledge of how to make it happen, and no guarantees whatsoever. It feels amazing. It's going to happen. We've turned the simple life of curb painting into something completely wild. Adam actually tears up one day, telling us how much this all means to him. Eden goes to him and hugs his leg, then Lightning too, which makes everyone laugh. We all stand in a circle on the upper patio, the evening upon us, and Gilles, mostly sitting this project out but definitely supportive, speaks up for the first time on all this film stuff.

"There is a magic here that moves through you all. Heather and I feel so fortunate to be here with you, in this moment. I'm no filmmaker, but I do know as sure as I stand here that the work you all are doing, as tough as it is, remember that you are standing on the shoulders of giants, all those filmmakers who came before you. The directors or whatever, I don't know their names, nobody does, but…"

"Steven Spielberg," I say, interjecting.

"Godard and Truffaut," says Dawn.

"George Lucas, Fritz Lang," chimes in Ed.

"Charlie Chaplin," adds Lightning.

"Okay, smartasses, let me finish." Stoned, Gilles smiles and drops his head down, our mockery of him just one more affectation of our love.

Before he can finish, Adam doubles down.

"Buster Keaton."

"Steve Martin, Richard Pryor," says Eve. Everyone chuckles as Gilles does a face palm, trying to hide his smile. Eve whispers something into Eden's ear, and she looks confused, but nails it.

"Alfred Hitchcock?" Eden says, putting her hands on her hips, as if scolding Gilles. A full round of laughter which takes a minute to get over.

"Okay, right. *Everybody* knows their names except me. The giants. Duh. But *anyway*, I want you all to know how special each and every one of you is to us." Heather lays her head on Dawn's shoulder. We all move into a circle as he reaches out to have us hold hands, a moment that will stay with me until the end of my days. A special kind of communication had formed in us, an answer to the problems we had back wherever each of us came from, forced into the present, this is one of those moments, where we all look upon each other, smiling and beaming with heart magic and love for each other. Hands still joined we raise them above our heads.

"Here's to the Gods of cinema, may they bless this film, and see it to completion, and great success." We all cheer. In proper New Orleans fashion, a marching band can be heard somewhere in the distance, getting ready to hit the road themselves.

The time for our departure comes. The planning is thorough, and we make our preparations and ship the boxes of costumes, props and various monster body parts back to New Mexico. We clean the house Saturday night, then depart the following morning, transported by a city bus down streets which become suddenly jammed with police cars and a giant crowd.

Lightning hangs out the window to ask a protestor, "Hey, what's going on?"

"Warrants getting served or something, I heard. Plus, there's this rally…"

On cue, here comes a march, blocking the intersection, people holding signs and using their civil rights to get the word out. As we sit and wait, gunshots ring out, and we watch, trapped on a bus, as people start to run in every direction. In addition to warrants being served and rallies for causes, rival street gangs have decided this morning is the time to settle turf battles as well.

We're caught in the middle of it as cops, gangs, and people from the nearby neighborhood, that all too rare group of protestors—housing activists, God bless them, the pre-dawn rabble rousers, eager for some headlines and column inches for their cause—decide to join in the summer fray, in a city trying to keep itself from getting fucked on a weekly basis by the powers that be. Not a moment too soon, our city bus veers off route, to the dismay of several passengers, but the driver isn't having any of it.

"You wanna go down on this bus, babies?" the driver yells. "Not me, not my ship! We changing routes!"

We got on the bus in silence and darkness only five minutes ago. Now, everyone's freaking out, literally. When we hear more gunshots, everyone hits the floor. I'm lying on the floor of the bus looking up as tear gas pours in the window and clouds the streets as cops try to vandalize the situation and the bus roars through a red light, almost tilting into Lake Pontchartrain. Everyone is yelling.

Then, as quickly as it started, the chaos becomes silence. The windows are all opened to let out the tear gas, people weep quietly, the bus engine now the only sound as everyone quits panicking and returns to their seats, the lake all around us as the sun climbs the horizon. The collective of commuters, graveyard janitors, late-nighters on their way down, and us; we all breathe a collective sigh of relief. We quickly reload our bus and hit the road. By lunchtime we're back on Texan soil. Good morning, America—how are ya?

18

FROM THE FEW NATIVE AMERICAN mythology books I could find, Amarok the monster, prevalent in Inuit mythology, was simply a giant wolf from the far north stalking and killing anyone foolish enough to be out at night. For our story I'd converted it into a giant half-wolf, half-bear, with the upright walk of a man. From Ed's renderings, it was a terrifying creature that rent limb from torso and found blood and organs most pleasant when spread upon its own body, adding an element of filth and revulsion that elicited gasps of sheer terror from anyone unfortunate enough to see one.

The sad part, the human element of an inhuman monster, that I most want to bring across in my script is that Amarok is called forth by another, and as such is a beast without agency. Pulled into this world by another, he kills and destroys at the caller's bidding, but is only dimly aware of what he is lacking, conscious of it. Like too many people, he too is simply a puppet. I want the character Ellie to be his ally, to be the only one who knows what he is, what he wants in this world.

We all take this work seriously, and our makeup and costuming attempt to reflect this. Late Sunday, we roll back into Four Corners. More curbs, this time in the less conspicuous nearby cities of Gallup, Bloomfield, and Aztec. The Southwest is blowing up in terms of suburban expansion, a thing we talk about one night around the fire.

"There's plenty of work right now, but we need to be cautious," Heather chimes in. "Cops asked me way too many questions about you all after the whole knife fight thing."

Adam nods reflectively, weighing decisions. "We'll make maps for the older neighborhoods. For now, keep to the established areas before we hit new subdivisions." We all agree.

Ed pipes in to change the subject. "We're still casting here in Farmington though, yeah?" Everyone looks to Adam.

"Don't look at me, I'm just the producer. You guys got this, right?" We all laugh at his fake incredulity. Adam keeps his nose in everyone's business.

Casting is the most difficult part of a film. Actors make or break a story, and when you're already dragging the river looking for corpses that you can reanimate, hopes don't get very high. Most of us are already actors in the film, and this requires a ton of work, as I'm now training amateur non-actors how to work on screen. I have some idea, as I worked several days on a TV movie set in the near past and try my best to get them up to speed.

Stoners are great, as they respond well to the *idea* of acting, and my encouragement inspires them. However, these are secondary players, so we'll still need to cast professionals, or at the very least trained people, or at the very very least not stoned people, for our protagonist and antagonist. Adam won't trust the lead role to a "dirt bag curb painter," and we've got few options, given our current living situation. His assessment of his compatriots leaves a bad taste in my mouth. His idea?

"Let's rent a room for a day at a hotel in Farmington and do our casting call there." Looks legit, feels like a real casting office. Dawn and I agree.

The Palermo is a historic hotel in the heart of Farmington. We choose the nicest room we can find and set it up to resemble what we believed a casting office would look like. A table for the producers (Dawn and Adam), a camera on a tripod, and a chair across from the camera to record the auditions. We print copies of the scenes we want read and lay them out, assuming this looks professional. I love the smell of freshly printed paper, from the mimeographed scents of my youth to the copiers of adulthood, just a whiff of that torched aroma can get me high. I've printed three copies of the final script and keep two close by at all times. As a kid, I vividly recall certain books held different smells. Paper printing is a delicate, aromatic process. I love paper.

For the last couple hundred years, newsprint littered the streets, homes, break rooms and bus benches across every city and country world-wide. Paper was the way to go. America's greatest and worst cities alike had them, fun titles like the *Queen Bee* and the *Plains-Dealer*, the *Daily Gazette* and the *Jimpelcute*. They were the lifeblood of any community, their constant connection to each other and to the world.

Comics. Sports stats. Opinion pages filled with commentary from well-educated and intelligent individuals, not today's screeching psychopaths with damaging ideas or racist ranters with axes to grind. I'm a voracious reader, and I love learning about the places I'm at and the world I live in through them. I grew up reading American newspapers, and even today never hesitate to pick one up, if one still exists for the place I'm passing by. Sometimes you find a little one like an *Auto Mart* cars-for-sale rag or a diminutive journal letting you know about the upcoming pancake breakfasts at the local grange hall. Want ads and personals ran the gamut from lost pets to desperately seeking to last minute airline tickets already printed for a one way to Hong Kong ready to be resold, cash only.

In Farmington, the stakes are no different from anywhere else, so we run an ad for casting, with the address at the KOA we're staying at and our phone number from the campground pay phone. The ad reads:

'Casting a horror film to be shot in the Four Corners area for 3-4 weeks in September. Looking for professional actors able to engage with original material. Please come prepared to do a scene with others. Résumé and head shot required.'

We thought, hoped - we might get twenty people to come out. Farmington is small but growing. We get almost a hundred auditions. And still, not a single film permit. Good Lord, we're going to get busted again. The city literally *just* told us to knock it off.

There is a Korean woman, Hae, who speaks no English but has an amazing audition. How she learned of us, I have no idea. She cannot speak or understand a single word of English, but clearly has a theater background. Her movements, her monologue in Korean, it's mesmerizing. She's so strange, so amazing and professional, while delivering her lines in her native tongue (the things she said we'll never know) and gives such a great, impassioned performance that when we meet her husband Dan, a former military guy from Houston, we realize there may be a way to do this. We hire her on the spot for the role of Native American Shaman. A true shaman speaks a universal language. No one'll know the difference. Dan speaks to her in Korean, and her face lights up when she realizes she got the job. It's feels good to make other people happy and be a part of making their dreams come true, too, no matter how crazy or small. We hand her an envelope stuffed with ones and fives, making it look like way more money than it is.

A man with pizza sauce on his shirt and pants sagging down around his ass gave a rendition from Easy Rider as his monologue: not hired. A wheelchair-bound man and his many children, all beautiful and electric. It was like somehow, we created the first reality show, and everyone within a hundred miles wanted in. The glut of amateurs, crazies, and professionals was unbelievable. Off duty firemen, hotel maids, and high school theater nerds all came, reaching for the stars. Take me, take me!

And then Jimmy Franks shows up. A real old-school theater actor, well into his fifties but tall and tan, muscular, a tight crew cut and posture to match. I think he thought there was some professional, NBC movie-of-the-week type-deal happening, seeming kind of let down when he sees us and our unprofessional appearances. He nails his monologue, however (A scene from Lawrence of Arabia, another film I've never seen), and Dawn not only knows the scene but speaks with him privately following his audition. Adam walks him out, returning a moment later, smiling.

"Yeah, that guy's in. He knows what he's doing. Plus, he sings and dances. Professionally."

"Maybe we should make a musical," says Dawn. She's onto something, but now's no time to lose focus. With so many choices we find ourselves in a pickle. Who can hack the environment we're about to throw them into, how well can they memorize lines and hit their marks? The noose was tightening, and Northern New Mexico was slipping into a late summer heat wave that left the general populace grimy, testy, and easily angered. The tension climbs as we creep ever closer to our first real shoot date: September 4th, 1990.

Like the true bad-ass he is, Lightning surprises us all when he returns one day with a bunch of used audio equipment to install into the bus, turning it into a traveling post-production audio studio. Thrift stores are all you need. Adam likes the idea but gives him very specific dimensions on where it can live in the bus (right behind the driver's seat, taking up no more than four by five feet). Space is limited, but he rises to the occasion and builds a fully operational miniature sound studio. He hides it all by covering it with a foam cutout that can attach to the wall with bungee cords and completely hide the system, making it look like it's just a piled-up bunch of clothes and garbage. Nothing to see here, folks.

Curb painting brings in a grip of cash, as long as you don't sit back on your ass and slow down. New Orleans was crucial for both rest and film prep, but our cash reserve have dropped too low. We cannot stop painting under any circumstances. And, because we are going to be allocating our best painters to making a movie for 3-4 weeks, we need trustworthy, hard-working kids who can handle the work, delegate responsibility to a crew of four or five people and do it all with very little oversight. And most importantly: to be trusted with hundreds of dollars in cash. This is a dangerous move. Remember, we ditch people often.

Just since I've joined the party, we've taken on ten to fifteen folks who then jumped ship or were kicked off. There are few anyone would trust to spearhead such a thing as an already established business that deals solely with cash. Yet we find just the guys, living out of their car with a trunk holding a shotgun and bowling balls, ready for whatever came next. We were it.

We're camped out on the edge of sagebrush country a couple miles east of Gallup. We had already distributed flyers and were camping close by, so we could be up bright and early to paint. We heard sounds coming from off in the chaparral, so we snuck over and found Taz and Caveman living out of the trunk of their car, their diet consisting of a gallon bucket of BBQ sauce they'd absconded with from the local McDonald's. Broke as shit, the end of the line.

We take them under our wings, feed them, and train them up as fast as we can. They take to curb painting like a reggae fan takes to Jimmy Cliff. We quickly realize that while we feel we can trust them, there's no sense in being stupid. Adam figures out their real names, where they're from, their parents' addresses, things the rest of us will never know. They're clean cut, all-American kids with looks that screamed 'I can be trusted.'

The curb painter style is dress for success. As opposed to most teenagers, we all look pretty weird. We were wild, and had been undomesticating ourselves for months, some of us years. Our scene was Mad Max meets Jesus Christ Superstar extras, and while Ed and I often go for the straight look, everyone else is steadfast in their commitment. A look may not define you, but a first impression is always key. And, at eight dollars an impression, I loved going square occasionally, even stoned. Ed often made his own clothes and once suited up, resembled a spaceman traveling through a psychedelic dreamscape. Put him next to Fred, who does door to door in khaki shorts, plain sneakers, no logo t-shirts and pulled back dreads. When these cats approach your door for eight bucks, you're initially confused but most are pleased and more than happy for the interruption. They're both incredibly handsome, did we mention that?

Taz and Caveman were fresh out of the system only a couple weeks, having just left Kansas and on the road to college in Arizona. Abruptly, they decided to abandon the obligation and follow the dream, the road dream, to claim the USA as their own, on their own terms. They had gone with their guts and bailed out, landing directly in our path, a perfect confluence of American outsider culture, old and new.

We bought them some used 'I'm trustworthy and probably go to church' collared shirts and within days, they *were* the team. With Eve as their foreman, they take the curb painting reins as we do final prep for shooting.

We cast a kid named Jo-Jo Turner from Farmington as our lead, the kid who touches the tainted mercury water and becomes the Amarok. Character name: Joe Dysentery. I learn a lot from a book on Guerrilla Theater from the seventies, which reveals how to cut corners in dramatic and theatrical ways without sacrificing art. We luck out again and cast an awesome 14-year-old kid named Francine to play Ellie, the Native girl who can speak to the monster. Her dad Frank comes along, and since he's the kind of guy who doesn't like to sit around, we give him the job of lead electrician. He tells us about something called gaff tape, a first for us. For some reason, he also knows about C-47s. We keep Frank in beer and sandwiches, he makes sure all our cables are wrapped and everything's plugged in and has batteries charged, simple little things that can get overlooked and slow down production.

We cast the firemen as our rich white developers. Heather, Morgan, Fred, and Gilles play the hippie gang, and a couple of recently retired cops from Durango drive down and play themselves, essentially, using their own police outfits, even though we're sure this is illegal. They didn't seem to care, so neither did we. We were so lawless it didn't matter, long as we got shit done.

Everything seems to be going so well, and yet? I'm starting to feel weird. My surface areas, my skin and nails start to feel, to look strange. They seem to have taken on a bluish sheen. My imagination is taking over. No one else seems to notice when I ask if "this looks weird to you?"

I have slipped into increasingly darker and more immoral thoughts. I've begun to fear the creature in my mind. Thinking like the Amarok and getting into his head allows him into mine, not the best idea for someone who is still partying and getting too little sleep, eating fast food and wandering the streets of America.

I don't want to succumb, but I have little choice. We need to make a movie.

19

FROM THE SURFACE OF THE EARTH, you wouldn't have seen see a thing. But as luck would have it, our late-night stoned desert wanderings that we so enjoyed led us to our greatest discovery. We're twenty miles from the nearest town, in a place that can be best described as 'total desolation.' We're camped south of Shiprock and as usual are camping on BLM land. We'd occasionally run into a rancher or kids shooting guns, but other than that—empty land. We're often hiking nearby hilltops and gulches, discovering Native pottery shards in the washes and gullies that crisscross the land, remnants of a broken culture.

On this particular afternoon, Dawn, Ed, Adam, Taz, Caveman and I wander toward the sound of a generator we can barely hear, deep in the chaparral. It's that same generator sound that comes from the killer's house in *The Texas Chainsaw Massacre*, but I keep my mouth shut about such cinematic parallels, and we forge on towards the source.

The humming machine grows louder and louder, and we eventually break out of the chaparral, spotting the generator, sitting next to a massive metal grate covering a large, dark hole. The generator is connected to a massive fire hose. One end snakes into the darkness of the earth, the other flooding the open plain we now stand in with water. Drainage is occurring, but drainage of what? Forty feet in diameter, this opening looks like something from another age, another time. We approach, cautiously. Just below the steel grated cover, there's a ladder mounted to the wall that snakes down hundreds of feet into the black. A platform there seems to allow access to the ladder, but the platform was a good ten feet below the surface of the desert. There's a slight hole, large enough for a single person, right in the middle where the hose escapes to pump water, and while we're all pondering the situation, Adam simply turns off the generator, it's so fucking loud.

"Should you do that?" asks Caveman. Adam looks around.

"Who's going to stop us? I couldn't hear myself think. We'll turn it back on when we leave." Adam says what I'm thinking: "We have to film this."

Dawn looks at me, smiling. Ed smiles a devil grin as he ties his hair back, the Eagle Scout preparing for what inevitably must come next.

"This is literally where the Amarok comes from, right? Let's do this." We grab the hose, now mostly empty as the generator was being used as a pump, and wrap it around the pipe structure above the hole and make our plan to slowly lower our first person in. We decide to do this in the approaching darkness of night, with cheap, dollar-store flashlights. The trickiest part is going to be sticking the landing on the platform just a few feet below the surface, a rusty, two-foot-wide metal plank, in a chamber forty feet around. A misstep in either direction is death.

We drop Ed in as our test subject, the guy who seems the least afraid of anything, ever. It's nightmarishly cool in that way that all forbidden places are. Flashlights pointed down through the rusty metal grating, we watch his descent with a great deal of nervousness and for the first time, I'm very much considering pulling back on this adventure. A sound from the bushes nearby turns our flashlights to the chaparral to which Ed patiently responds, "please shine the light down." He hasn't hit the landing yet and we've given him no light to work with.

"Dude, it's bottomless!"

As Ed hits the platform, his touchdown reverberates into the void, an echo into darkness.

"It's *really* deep. I can't see the bottom."

Taz is the first to voice concern, looking down on Ed with a 'we should be careful' face.

"Are we really climbing in there? How the hell are we going to get out?"

"Ah, what's the worst that can happen?" Adam says, sizing up the gravity of moving forward. We all laugh and rattle off a laundry list.

"Fall to our deaths?" says Dawn, a look of comic fear on her face. Taz offers another possibility.

"Get stuck in the bottom and starve to death?" We all laugh nervously, no one wanting to be the weak link that chickens out. Cave Man adds what should be the most unreasonable option.

"Maybe we'll get eaten by something trapped down there, waiting for idiots like us to drop into its lair?"

Dawn checks her watch. "Well, it *is* feeding time..."

Each of us tougher than the last, we shrug off the negative possibilities. One after the other, we slip down the deflated fire hose to the platform and then descend the three-hundred-foot ladder that is mounted to the wall to the bottom, where a two-foot-thick door has been propped open.

Ed does the once around, sizing up the situation.

"You guys know what this is, right?" Adam smiles, always ready with the answers.

"Sure, it's a nuclear missile silo. We used to break into one back in Texas, drink beers down there. They're everywhere; the missiles were removed and this one was obviously flooded to keep people like us out."

Passing by the massive door, Caveman looks back.

"Man, someone closes this door, we're fucked."

We all laugh, hiding our fears and leaning into the adventure.

"We have to film here!" Dawn takes the lead, running ahead of everyone into the vast main entrance, excited. "It's like an alien ship!" she cries out, echoing into the abyss as she comes running back down the long-abandoned hallways towards us, shining her light back and forth at all the rooms that cut off the main corridor.

The place was indeed flooded, walls and ceiling still covered in moisture for what appears to have been a very long time and now, for some reason, recently drained. We explore the living quarters. The words "no smoking in bed" are stamped in fading letters on the damp walls.

Conference rooms and command centers are caked in rust, ancient terminals and endless corroded panels, swollen, misshapen computer boards full of caked, frozen knobs and discolored buttons, like a rotting spaceship that's been traveling through an ocean of emptiness, alone and untended for millenia.

Everything about it was at once awesome and terrifying. We know the dangers, but we're cocky about them—until the sound.

"I'm sure I imagined it," Ed says, and then we all hear it. A splash, somewhere nearby.

Fear, genuine and sharp, grabs my gut. Sound is the darkest and most terrifying harbinger of bad things to come. Now would be a great time to, like my long-ago babysitter, hit mute and continue the trek in silence. I wouldn't be half as scared, regardless of what may be around the corner, if I couldn't hear it.

To be hundreds of feet underground in a rusty nuclear missile silo and hear something moving is not a problem if you don't believe in monsters. We just climbed several hundred feet into the earth, walked half a mile into some primordial death trap, only one way out—and then the sound. Nothing else could possibly be here, right? We hear it again, a splash and then a dragging, metallic sound, and decide it's time to exit, quickly.

All good horror movies misdirect viewers by using sounds that could very well be normal creaks and groans, the sounds of a normal, working world until at last, you realize it's something else. See: Alien, 1979. Something alive, and hungry. That kind of sound.

We all huddle together, realizing the low scraping noise that needs immediate attention seemed to be coming from the direction we need to go, back to the entrance. It was distant, but there's no way around. We need to go forward. Can a group of people all imagine the same sound? This was a foolish and ill-advised plan. Two of our three flashlights die within several minutes. We move quickly.

The dragging, scraping echoes follows us as we pass through decrepit hallways and burned out, cavernous rooms. We hit a dead end then turn back once, twice. Dawn, to my surprise, is genuinely afraid. She takes my arm, holding tighter than I think she realizes.

"Damnit. There is definitely something else down here. Keep moving." The fear is getting the best of us, a group of eager, confident roustabouts, once fearing nothing and now facing the one thing we all fear: the dark.

I wonder if it's something in the air. Is it possible it's in one of us now and using us as an escape device? A virus that senses the possibility of freedom to do more damage and has somehow escaped into my lungs, or my blood. Am I a carrier?

We finally make the door, then the ladder, climbing one by one out of the darkness into the safety of a midnight desert, never so happy to see the sky and stars. We fire up the generator, returning it to its deafening job, and as the water begins to pump once more, covering our tracks, we laugh and try to shake off the shudder as we trek back to the campfire to relay our grand adventure to the rest of the family. No one believes a single word.

The next morning, before anyone's awake, Dawn and I return to the silo, ahead of the day's shoot. We'd turned the generator back on when we left the previous evening, but the gas ran out overnight, and it's pleasantly quiet. A small lake has pooled around the silo entrance, and birds congregate and drink. We arrive just as the sun rises, catching sight of wild mustangs taking their fill at this new lakeshore. They see us but seemed disinterested by our presence and quietly return to drinking. I put my arm around Dawn's shoulder as we watch in silence, the deafening beauty climbing into my heart.

There are moments that can change a person for all time. I know someday, sooner or later, this will all end, and I'll move into another phase, another way. Maybe I would finish college. Maybe I would make more monster movies. Maybe I'd go overseas and become a cabinet maker with a guy named Thor in Leicester Square, working my days away, growing old and spending endless evenings taking in films at the Prince Charles Cinemas. In any of these possibilities, I knew I'd never return to my life as it was before I'd been found and spirited away.

Magic can't, shouldn't, last forever. That morning in the desert, a beautiful human by my side amidst shooting a film of desperate economic conditions, when everything seemed always about to collapse, I'd never felt more untethered, like the mustangs across our pond: unburdened and skittish, but free.

20

MONDAY MORNING. We cut Taz and Cave Man loose to do some damage in town while we hike Amarok body parts and our actors back to the silo site. We're improvising as many shots as we can of the beast coming up from underground, the Shaman calling the beast into existence, as many pick-ups as we can before we get caught. We know the site won't stay abandoned forever, so it's a hustle. Sucess prevails when we reach our actors by payphone the previous night and have them hustling there, reminding us how lucky we are. Everyone here believes in the power of blood.

<u>Original Recipe:</u>

Fake blood: A concoction of desperate economic times. Serves 4-6.

1. Be cheap. Think big, but if your recall of old monster magazine recipes doesn't work, and there's no library nearby to reach out to, go to the Farmington local suopermarket. That's right, that's how they spell it because it's owned and run by Latinos who screwed up their giant signage initially, but to their surprise it became a draw and it's an awesome market in any case and it would ruin it if they tried to fix it, so yeah. Go to Suopermarket and hit the baking aisle.

2. Don't get distracted by the panderia on your way down the main aisle, just go find the azucar. They'll probably stock Karo syrup, but any liquid sugar is fine. Buy it all because you'll need it, sixty-six cents a bottle. Grab a couple big boxes of cornstarch as well.

3. Suopermarket has it all. There's an actual hairdresser in the back, giving haircuts and styles as people shop for food. On the shelves just outside her little glass-walled back room you'll find hair supplies. Grab cheap red and black hair dye. Again, buy it all, several bottles of each to cover all the gruesome gore you'll be creating and then some.

4. Buy (2) giant plastic buckets, (2) whisks, the longest plastic spoons or ladles you can trash and throw away. Grab duct tape and disposable latex gloves too.

5. At your campground table, in a giant bucket mix several bottles of syrup and whisk away as you slowly add red and black hair dye at intervals to make the color you believe is best. Cornstarch should be used sparingly as it tightens up the blood quick. Minimal amounts according to overall volume. Water thin for spraying on people's faces, thicker for pooling around a dead corpse. Go with your gut, keep it dark.

Prepare your desired mixtures as close to the rolling of cameras as possible. It's a mess, so you'll want to get it mixed and runny right at shoot time. The weather is of course wildly fluctuating, for us it was early fall on the Colorado Plateau, so depending on the time of day you shoot it could be eighty degrees or it could be twenty. A good mix can be a struggle to hold. As blood tech, your task is to get people excited when they see your work. It's the backbone of a monster movie, when life becomes death, and if you get it right, bravo. Well made

Actors arrive fired up on coffee and donuts, the heat wave now broken, and we shoot a whole day there. We all recognize the opportunity, so we're shooting tons of footage of all these crazy, starkly lit interiors; the darkness from below, the light from above—I have too many ideas for a twenty-hour shoot. I envision much of this footage can be used on other films in the future. No art department could adequately capture the creepiness, the absolute character of this location, so shoot shoot shoot, you sons of bitches!

All morning we go at it. Lightning, Adam, and I hang from the ladder at various depths with cameras strapped tight, extra belts and ropes wrapped around us and attached to the rails to keep us from falling to our deaths so we can get a shot of the gangly, grotesque arms of the Amarok reaching up into our world, out of the darkness, a thing from somewhere far below, unannounced and unknown. We shoot late into the afternoon, always expecting to have someone arrive and bust us at any minute. They never come.

We rehearse that evening under a starry sky in the warmth of a southwestern Indian summer; the production's confidence keeps energy high. Our Shaman Hae has brought her husband Dan along and he continually provides us with sandwiches, chips, and cold sodas from a massive cooler.

The underground silo sequences remain my favorite from the shoot. Group shots are fun, simple two-shot dialogues are plain yet crucial and we use early Soviet-style close ups for conversations, coming close for eye-to-eye movement, the language of the face so superior to words. But down in that hole, everything was marked by the tension and danger of the space: nuclear war, the total annihilation of humanity was literally once possible from right here, and it brought a sketchy energy to the scenes we filmed.

With flashlights and cheap white poster boards we bounce and cut light in the most creative ways, multiple takes of Joe Dysentery's original touching of the nuclear-tainted water, despite the warnings of Rainbow. Down in that abysmal hole I learned how to pull focus, how to use a light meter and make spot-on assumptions, how to hold and stabilize a camera in a myriad of situations, from standing ankle-deep in tainted, possibly nuclear waste-water (barefoot, no less) to capturing moments of true fear and confusion to hanging off ledges, shooting into the abyss, light descending in needle-thin shafts into black hole earth; I was so proud of those shots and the power of the images. I twist my moustache into long spikes as we ready another take.

"Action!" yells Dawn from above. The camera rolls as the monster's arm reaches into frame, yearning to be free, to kill. The Amarok, its purest wish to extract revenge on beings foolish enough to tempt fate and destroy the earth, a simple monster with simple desires. Pulling apart our poorly constructed prop arms and having our little blood tubes rip perfectly and let the red stuff spray across actor's faces as they scream in horror, man —

it doesn't get any better than that. It's the kind of thing that makes one never want to yell "Cut!"

After two full days of shooting at the silo and in the chaparral nearby, the family gets so many returns for address numbers in town, we all need to jump in and get them painted in one morning. Crew and actors alike throw in to get the cash flowing again, all except Hae and Dan, who head to a spa for the day. Dawn and I split off the next morning after painting alone and hit some dumpsters, always searching.

Dawn prefers foraging for her feasts and finds the most amazing things, a first-class dumpster diver, a ferret who plunders the waste of strip malls, grocery stores, and pizza parlors, always coming up with something useful or at least cool. She can see what lies within from outside, our unofficial procurer of all items crucial and weird. Sometimes it's cold pizza from the Round Table, others it's frozen shark steaks and hard blocks of sherbet ice cream from Safeway. Faded, well-cut western shirts and old, unused clutches of socks from the Silver Saddle western wear outlet, cases and cases of "expired" water ditched out back of the Farmington community services district offices. She makes the idea seem easy and fun, diving into gross, reeking dumpsters that house the supposed wastes of society, only to find things often coveted, somehow knowing the value of even the most obscure book that she plunders.

"Oh, shit—*In Dubious Battle* by Steinbeck. Look at this date!" She flings the book at me. "Prolly a first edition." I try to catch the books as she flings them out. The spinning spines make comedic spirals as they fly; she's like some ravenous text-devouring creature, making funny guttural noises as she works, well aware of how it all looks outside the bin. We are always creating absurdist theater for ourselves.

"What the hell is going on in there?" I call out, laughing. "You find any condoms?"

A sharp laugh from within, her deep snort brings a smile to my face as she pops up like a puppet and winks at me, immediately disappearing again. She is processing materials, assessing value, then flinging them into the world, free once more, rescued from the landfill. The Steinbeck was in a bag of romance novels, inside a bag of clothes, tossed into the dumpster she's currently wading through in the hot midday sun behind an old bookstore. She's constantly digging down deep to get to the bottom to stay on top.

We spend our rare quiet moments together, reading out loud our favorite passages from the books on the shelves of the same little bookstore, located in downtown Farmington when we finish painting early, which is almost always. We buy nothing, but the store owner doesn't seem to care.

That afternoon, when we're supposed to be collecting money, we start making out in the darkened aisles of medicine and science, pages and tongues, flesh and bindings. The mixture of scents, our passions and the stench of yellowing pages, is intoxicating. Suddenly, she roughly pins me into the biography section and slides my hand into her skirt, pulling my hair back so she can devour my neck, my fingers find her reception warm and inviting. She glances quickly to the front—no one around for pages and pages—and we fall into the corner and down into the warm, faded carpet where no one can see, except the old gallery of books and stories all around us. Galley alley.

I'm on top of her and she closes her eyes, reaching out and grabbing a book at random as I undo her dress, a corpulin of clips and tiny hooks. Her dress is loose and sliding down her legs, boots off, the energy positively electric. She giggles as I nuzzle her with my new-found moustache and scruff that makes me feel dirtier and more beatnik than ever. Her dark locks spread out on the old, faded carpet like a mandala cast in shag and cinders. I've never been so close to losing myself in someone. She begins to read a passage selected quickly, without thought, from the randomly seized book. A real pants-off affair. She glances at the cover.

"From Steven Pinker's *The Language Instinct,*" she proclaims.

"'Ordinary speech, like color, vision or walking, is a paradigm of engineering excellence. A technology that works so well its user takes its outcome for granted…'" Flushed, she looks deep into my eyes as she can feel me about to part the curtain and take my place, center stage, all foot lights up and flickering no more.

Solid light streams from all around, not just above but from all angles, no more shadows, and then a gasp emits from my paragon of compatriotism, gone girl all and a shining goddess in her stead, glowing and rising to meet me. "'…unaware of the complicated machinery'—oh fuck yeah- *Ohhhummmm*— 'hidden behind the panels.'"

Eyes closed, I have a vision just then of everything to ever come, good and bad, wrong and right, mistakes made and rectified, lovers come and gone, a future far away and lost in my mind's eye. It lasts half a second and then, my turn at invocation. A random choice.

"Grab a book," she whispers, "do your summoning."

We open our eyes, deep in our sections, lost in the endless aisles of stories awaiting their fate, a private moment. Not looking away, I reach up and grab a book of my own, a small paperback, and do the same. Unknown and untitled. My invocation. Just flip it open and read.

"'The horror which possessed my young fancy'"—we both laugh at this line then quickly glance to the front of the store—

"'-was beyond anything I have ever experienced.'" She flips the cover to show me the title.

The Principles of Psychology by William James. Smiling with sex, sweat, and syntax, her eyes rolled back, she removes her shirt and starts on mine, rising up to lick my torso as she goes. The eternal pages of the psych section look down in glowing approval. The show of Magdalene ages, where pages are all the rages, finally free of all their bindings.

"Continue, please," she moans, the slight hum in her throat keeping me hard and focused.

"'The head was covered in a long black veil which floated out into the moonlight…'"

Her tongue continues to cross my chest and neck in long swirls. I am so turned on right now that I can only read in the faintest of breathless whispers.

"'The face itself was pale and beautiful, and the lower part swathed in the white band commonly worn by the nuns of Catholic orders.'"

I look down at Dawn's narrow waist and see a small white cord around it. She wears this all the time, but now its meaning is loaded and crazy. In my mind's eye, I see it as the cord that binds us, the cable that runs through and ties me to her, not unlike some darker magic that in all probability I have completely misread.

She leans back, I lay the book down to really do my part here, but she stops me and pulls my ear to her mouth so she can whisper.

"Finish the invocation…" She grabs a small book from a bottom shelf and splays it open across her forehead, puts her hands together as if in prayer, making her look, with the white cord, like the sexiest Catholic school girl/Mad Max runaway I've ever seen, will ever see.

"'For a time, I grappled with my superstitious terrors, then decided to not turn away but rather to lean into the fear, and I realized that I actually believed in the reality of the apparition, since I have not, by the slightest word, exaggerated the vividness of my feelings.'"

Books closed. Time's up. Pencils down.

As quietly as possible we fuck, sweaty and primal, thrusting on musty carpet in the psychology section in the back corner of a used bookstore on a Tuesday afternoon in Farmington New Mexico, 1990. Because who wouldn't? We came to party, and party is what we did. The bell over the front door rings and we lay, waiting, hoping that someone won't walk around the corner and find us naked on the floor. Not a sound but the birds outside.

The sunlight shifts in the window, time catches up, then passes. Minutes of post-coital kissing and licking the cum off of each other because we're dirty and clean in unity and we're sexy creatures, sexy enough to taste ourselves on each other, and then it's over.

All moments must end. If they didn't, they wouldn't be moments. The clothes come back on and as we quietly exit a seemingly empty store, Dawn swipes a book from the rack at the door, a title I will always remember and never, ever read: *The Queen of the Damned*. We were growing increasingly closer. Or so I thought.

21

EVERYTHING FEELS DEADLY important now. The imperative to finish is hanging on us all. Summer is almost done, and the tight frost of early mornings has alerted us to the change coming. For some, it's a "let's finish this shit and move on" scenario. For others, it's the greatest thing that's ever happened in our lives. Curb painting has become a full-blown affair whereby we need more vehicles to house our growing team.

Amarok (official title now) is in full production, meaning every day is either shooting, rehearsing, or a million other various production jobs that we learn exist by simply running up against them. Costumes need to fit. Makeup is crucial. Lighting is critical. Little filmmaker arguments spring up throughout our days, a special communication in a language we're just learning. Dawn and Adam are constantly at it.

"The sun flared on that shot, I think we need to reshoot it."

"No—that's a lens flare. A lens flare is good, looks cool."

"I don't think you value my opinion."

"Well, I don't think *you* want to finish this shot list today."

On a whim, Dawn sends publicity stills to *Famous Monsters* magazine, who is hosting a contest. It could be great press. We're naïve enough to believe a bunch of homeless desert rats high on drugs and life can make a feature from nothing and hold it up to the respectable world of cinema and monster magazines everywhere will embrace it with fascination and acclaim. The footage thus far does look great, but the shoot struggles to be the film we envision. Because it's video, we watch our little version of dailies at the room we've rented downtown, just a deck plugged into a little hotel room TV. This creates a little schism in our group, as several of us get to stay in beds while the rest are sleeping in the bus or on the ground.

And now, Adam constantly drives little wedges between the three of us and the rest of the family. Maybe he sees us as usurpers of the throne, or something dishonorable and wants to keep us down and sow dissent (us in the hotel, them in the bus). He doesn't want the family to love us or need us more than they need him; some people are wired for distrust. What's pissing him off is that it's not working.

Eve and I still hit it off, I know he doesn't get a lot of our jokes, so maybe it's as simple as that. Literal-minded people are wired for suspicion and doubt. His observations are simple, petty comments.

"Man, who's in charge here?" he says, while Dawn and I try to get a particular conversation between the shaman and Ellie locked in at an abandoned trailer outside town.

"We don't have all day, guys. We making a movie here or what?" Shit like that.

He's doing that weird power thing where he's started to believe he's better than the rest. He is the producer, but man—don't make people feel like dirt. He too is changing. We all are. Today I get angrier than I've been, a monstrous anger, swelling up as he rattles on, slowing the progress of the day. It doesn't help that I've been drinking warm beers since ten a.m.

Something I'm just now learning about art, real art you will never capitulate on, nor fail to see through to its inevitable conclusion, is that it fundamentally changes you, turns you. If we're not careful, we may all be turned into something we'll regret.

"Seriously, shut the fuck up." I say and spit in Adam's direction when he interrupts too many times. He quiets down and walks away. Ed and Dawn smile. This is the first time I've confronted him to his face. It won't be the last.

Dawn drops some photos with a letter inquiring about work at the magazine, into a postal box downtown. It's windy today and our fingers are stained with the black and white palette that defines our existence, along with speckles of the reflective glass beads that make our address numbers the best.

"Fairy dust hands," says Dawn, and it always hurts. We use the cheapest supplies available, and we become that which we do. Nail polish remover helps, but that eats away at your hands as well. It never leaves you. The van comes by at the pick-up point and we shoot back across town with our crew of painters and actors and immediately get down to a very important evening: night shoots.

Our young actors do well in close spaces like the bus and trailers, arguing and fighting through their scenes, repeating my dialogue, sometimes actually line for line. As the cameras roll and the crew works, I watch our stars hit their marks and bring my words to life. I can't help but believe in magic, the effect of text, of incantation and the ability to turn someone into something new.

INT. BUS - NIGHT

                    RAINBOW
          You can't just tell a medicine man
          what to do! He has the ability to,
          to, to...

Rainbow is at a loss for words, tripping out.

Francine paces the bus, holding her head with both hands.

                    FRANCINE
          Fuck. Something has to be done.
          That thing has to be stopped.

CROSS FADE TO

EXT. DRY WASH - SUNRISE

Developer GLEN runs through the wash, sun about to break the
horizon. His clothes, tattered. His gait, broken. He is
sweaty and injured, struggling to climb a small rise, away
from the arroyo.

                    GLEN
          Gotta get out of here...

He staggers to the top and looks back, hearing it in the
trees coming for him, just out of sight.

CLOSE UP ON HIS FACE

                    GLEN (CONT'D)
               (whispers)
          What are you?

He stays put to watch it emerge from the tree line, fifty
yards away.

                    GLEN (CONT'D)
               (yelling)
          WHAT ARE YOU?!

A roar unlike any he's ever heard echoes across the
landscape. We see trees rustling, and then our first real
look at the monster.

It walks, stilt-like, out of the trees. Its misshapen head
sways side to side as it lumbers forward. A terrifying
creature, twice the height of a human, with an exposed rib
cage, impossibly alive and hungry. Looking directly at Don,
it's eyes glow. Blood and guts covers the outside of its
body.

Glen turns and runs. The Amarok leans forward, moving faster than looks possible for such a misshapen thing.

> GLEN (CONT'D)
> Dear God, somebody help me! I don't
> want to die! I want to live!
> Please!

He stumbles, again and again, coming to rest after twisting his ankle against the only thing completed in the new development, a beautiful wooden sign with a Native American motif sign that says 'Desert Winds - your new luxury home!'.

The Amarok is within twenty feet now, a club footed stagger/run that threatens to overcome Glen in seconds.

Suddenly, the low human howl of ELLIE. We see her with megaphone in the distance, calling to the beast.

The Amarok turns to look at her. Glen sees Ellie also and watches her, holding out hope that maybe this is his savior.

A moment of COMMUNICATING BY EYES, *close ups on both Ellie and the Amarok eyes*, before it turns away. Vengeance cannot be stopped.

Eat the rich. Ellie watches as Glen is caught, then shredded into a useless pile of meat, pressed slacks and guts. Blood sprays everywhere, leaving a pool of red swirling around Native pottery shards in the wash.

By shooting on video and watching footage daily, repeated mistakes are becoming less and less as we bungle along, learning first-hand. I miss the camaraderie that surely exists in film school programs across the world, places where artists and students make daily strides in a much more professional manner, making far superior films than us. I envy that scene and know I could be there if I had made even a small effort to apply myself to those programs. I lament, then smoke a joint (our last) with Lightning to relax. The weed in those days was so lightweight, so minimal in its effect that I loved to smoke a couple throughout the day. It was a nice high, a gentle touch from the cosmos that allowed one to open the mind a bit past what we're normally wired for.

I get the sense, deep inside my monster fried brain, that what we're doing is right. Making a film with cinema virgins and road dogs, hitchhiking conspiracy theorists, punked-out vagabonds and dumpster divers, wide-eyed mystical idiots and hard-working roustabouts with no jobs to go to or bills to pay, all this I reflect on makes it clear: these are my people. I could be in no better place than be here now. Namaste, motherfuckers.

Everyone fawns over Dawn and her directing abilities, she's the nuts and bolts of the project, and while she protests complimentary language, it's clear she loves this gig. We love her for the work she does, the energy she commits, and the clarity of her direction, but who wouldn't? We're her comrades, her lovers and sisters and brothers.

And now, the important scenes to shoot before we get the hell out of dodge: one chase scene through alleys and back streets, a mob scene, intent on destroying the monster, and a rooftop scene that serves as our big crane shot at the end. I know it is totally unreasonable and dangerous to try and shoot from the top of the highest building in town without permission, but I know what these shots do. I've seen too many great films that either open or close on a big overview of the worlds we're about to enter or now leaving. I must have it. The rooftop of the Farmington Motor Inn will be mine. Also, a chase scene. Why on earth did I write a chase scene?

We get a bunch of Farmington residents, for twenty bucks apiece, to commit to sitting in abandoned old offices at a warehouse across town that will double as our city hall, then lighting torches and running down the street yelling for revenge. On paper it looks great but shooting these scenes will be challenging enough when one knows what they're doing. Never mind if you've never done it before. So, we watch movies.

162

Luckily, Adam, Dawn and I practiced a few rogue road shoots in New Orleans. We knew the scene where the angry mob, eager to slay the beast, light torches (a whole other technical and legal issue) and run into traffic was going to be tricky and would require the commitments of our entire group. We need everyone on board on this one. Having a hard time trying to educate the others on the mechanics of chase scenes, I go back to square one. VHS.

We have to forge an ID card to get a membership at the local video rental, Farmington's own Video Chest, since we don't have an address. We spring for a cheap TV and VCR, already having a converter to run them by car battery at our campground as we've run out of money for stupid stuff like hotel rooms. We drag the equipment fireside, running everything off the bus battery, to let everyone watch the mother of all "how to make a film" films, *Raiders of the Lost Ark*. We gather around the fire as Ed props the TV on a picnic table and hits play on the VCR.

"See how the people run past the camera as it tracks in the other direction, not looking at it?" I hold the remote, pausing at certain scenes, making sure we're all learning, not just being entertained.

Watching this film, by campfire, under the stars, everyone is engaged and now learning alongside us. We're all filmmakers, all actors, all artists. No hierarchy, no leaders, no fakers, just workers and makers. Eve oversees the extras, and makes no bones about doing the job.

"Actors, schmactors. These people will run and scream if I have to light them on fire myself." She grabs a flaming log from the fire, waving it around for dramatic effect.

Local men whom we've cast as extras get us a line on some great weed, something we've been out of for a couple of weeks. Adam jumps at the chance and immediately he's gone with them to get a ¼ pound from a girl out in who-knows-where. He's gone overnight but returns the next day with the goods. And the dealer.

Her name's Marty, and she seems a little sketchy, but Adam says we're bringing her on board. For one thing, she never really looks anyone in the eyes. Shifty people make the family nervous. Eve is clearly not cool with this, she seems to know Marty, but there it is.

The campfire that night rages as no one's been high for a bit and everyone really cuts loose. Super fun, except for Eve, who fumes in the bus. Then, one of the actors gets Eden high when he accidentally lets her eat a mushroom, just a cap, but for a little kid that's a Class A Bad Move. Eve loses her shit and beats the guy up. Next morning, he's gone. Screw him. We're totally committed to getting this thing in the can. No one will fucking stop us.

Four in the morning, stars still out, I rise and wander into the desert, a late-night rainstorm now past, the sky promising blue soon, stars spill like milk across the end of night. I had read a lot of beat literature and poetry before getting Shanghaied in Oakland, but now I've drifted to crime novels and dollar-rack thrillers; engaging yet utterly forgettable. It's the beginning of a new chapter in my reading career—useful garbage. Whatever I still can do I will. I must. I drag out the typewriter and start a new story, just in case.

The camera has been acting funky, the result of being stored for the most part in fluctuating temperatures and in dry, sandy conditions.

"That stuff's cheap, buy another one," says Adam. Eve pulls the purse strings, and Adam is on thin ice with her anyway, and she has an immediate, terse response.

"Fuck that. We'll get it fixed." She grabs the camera and stomps out of the bus.

Eve and I take the camera to town, shelving another day of shooting. Adam's behavior has turned erratic since the arrival of Marty. He seems to be less engaged with the film, and more involved with her. He doesn't notice anything's wrong at all, no awareness of a shifting of energies. As a family, we're all watching him, waiting to see how this unfolds.

Every medium sized town in America once had a guy who could fix and rebuild anything, from lawn mowers and cars to VCRs and movie cameras. Sam's Cameras was one of the last bright stars in a constellation of repair shops scattered across a country that once made heroic efforts to hold everything together and made everything go. It's glue like Sam's shop that keeps our heads above water. Once you remove the middleman and make people throw away fixable things, you're basically saying *fuck the people*, make them spend money they don't have, make trash we can't get rid of. These are the thoughts that run through me as I reflect on our filmmaking dilemmas.

There's no escaping the horror of the real world, so much more imaginably terrible than a cursed, ragged beast killing a bunch of unlucky construction workers and their capitalist overlords. This is a collective,

American problem. Though it's definitely happening more and more in industrialized countries across the globe, America started this shit. We freedom-talking, patriotic fuckers are to blame the minute we start throwing away repairable things, the second we make trash and garbage for a future generation who will have no fucking clue how to deal with it. We're doomed, all of us, the whole human race; I have no doubt that humanity, in the end, will burn like film stuck in a projector. Without our precious technology to save us, all will eventually melt in front of a light too bright to bear, the story never finished. At least some great stories were told. The day and a half wait on the camera was painful, but now at least we have another ally—the repairman.

Taz, Caveman, and I paint a small neighborhood on the north side of Gallup to get a little more money in the bank. We earn a pitiful forty bucks for a day's work, and this gives us little more than the cost of the clean and repair job on the camcorder. We stock up on toilet paper, rice, beans, and tortillas and head back to camp. The cheap bottle of tequila, Eve stashes in her purse. No sense telling everyone.

The actors are coming apart, trying to hang in there with us but our scene is a mess and challenging at best for people from the straight world. When production shuts down, they're forced into either curb painting, hanging around the camp all day, or watching the kids and, inevitably, they grow restless. Tensions heighten around camp and that some have started to call bullshit on our efforts is creating divisions and factions. Hae and Dan have the privilege of simply leaving and staying in the nearest hotel. Why and how they hung in there throughout the anarchy, I cannot decipher.

"Call when you need us, we'll be in town."

"Will we finish this film?" Joe asks. I'm afraid to answer. Jimmy Franks drives out tonight to what he believed to be his final day of acting as one of the developers, but instead is greeted with no cameras, no lights, and an abandoned set. He's never done a film, but as a performer with over thirty years of experience under his belt, he knows how to do what we need him to do, and in truth he knows it better than us, senses it, and listens well. Jimmy hits his marks, knows how to project, he can do fear, anger, laughter—pretty much anything. But it's obvious he looks down on us. We're literally passing a joint around as he speaks. He laughs and shakes his head.

"What have I got myself into? Jesus." He demands his daily rate: 25 bucks for today, just for all the advice he gave us.

The girl who plays our lead hippie girl, Rainbow, is able to cool him down with her charm and convince him to return, but it's clear: we're going to have to pay him to keep him on board, work or no work. I pay him out of Dawn's boot and he leaves, hopefully sticking to our agreement that the camera and the monster will be ready for his death scene, next Friday. I later take the opportunity to remind everyone of the lesson here tonight.

"He's right. We know nothing. If we listen to guys like that, every day we'll get better and better." What I really need is for the team to listen, to hear my words. Alas, I feel it slipping away.

Egos are the first to go in film, and his constant verbal jabs and deteriorating faith in the project have us all seeing clearly what he cannot: Alpha Adam is having a hard time checking his at the door.

22

DAYS LIKE THIS are fun but exhausting. We start at six or seven, trying to knock off when the sun gets too hot, then wait for late afternoon to shoot the rest of the day's list, often until ten or eleven. One day, as we're getting one of the best takes of the film so far, the beast pursuing Don across a barren landscape, about to seal his fate, a large herd of goats storm through the shot, with no herder in sight. Jimmy Franks, playing the developer Don, hesitates, unsure what to do. Dawn and Taz, Amarok's other puppeteer/operator, move forward under the Amarok as if nothing's wrong.

"Keep rolling!" Dawn cries out, camera still rolling as we move in on the goats from another angle to frighten them, so they scatter as if from the sight of the monster. It works perfectly, as opposed to everything going on off screen. Film life, great. Curb life, starting to fray. Dawn, Ed, and I converse privately about stealing our film back, wresting it from the grip of the son of God. He provided all the tools necessary to make it happen, and now he's off with some girlfriend? What about his wife and kid? What about this movie? We hold a secret team meeting of three to discuss finishing the film.

"Mutiny is the last thing I want, but this ship is listing," Ed laments.

Dawn is worried Adam will flip out, and really, where would we go? How would we finish without our band of maniac castaways? What would we do without them?

She cracks her neck and spits on the ground.

"Our job is to finish this film. Leave Adam to me."

Our focus is like a dream now, unable to do much more than fight for its survival. What's she going to do, stab him?

Today, as we paint curbs in a nice neighborhood, Adam and Eve show up unannounced with strange children who run all over the place. Whose children they are, we don't know, there's no other adults. What did they do, raid a day care? As usual, Adam has an answer for everything.

"We're watching these kiddos for a couple days while our friends up in

Colorado, another curb painting team, paint a couple neighborhoods outside Silverton."

"Great," responds Dawn. "How about keeping them out of the street?"

Kids are everywhere, and it's uncomfortable. People driving by watching us, people looking out their windows, the judging eyes now coming down on us. The pure tension of this scene, to be on formerly quiet suburban streets suddenly arguing about a movie shoot with kids running into traffic, all anarchic and weird energy, is palpable. No one wants their curb painted by fifteen people, it's just too weird. It's like a cult arrived on your front lawn, bad juju. And then, on cue, here come the cops.

This time, it's serious. Turns out, Adam's new girl Marty is indeed a wanted runaway, and apparently a thief. Luckily, she's back at camp but now we're expected to hide her identity from the cops if they come looking for her, which Adam seems to think will happen. Later that evening, the cops do indeed come to our camp site and catch her trying to hide under the bus. We all watch as they take her away in handcuffs. There's nothing illegal about living this life out here, but when you're running from warrants the road to freedom is perilous. We build a small fire, ignoring the black storm clouds on the horizon, everyone a mixture of fatigue, despair and gloom.

"Well, at least she's gone," says Lightning. Thunderstorms follow, and rain comes on for days, not only freezing but monsoon-like, too. The sun disappears into the west, and we're left flooded and dark.

168

23

MONSOON SEASON fluctuates wildly in the American Southwest. You can get hit with a brutal storm surge in March, black clouds punched through with bright sunlight and eighty-degree temperatures on the freeways of Phoenix, forcing you to stop your vehicle and seriously consider abandonment.

The end of August can similarly bring a flash flood warning across New Mexico that sounds like a disaster alert on the radio, and it is. Head for high ground. Water rises in minutes and can kill you fast. There's no joking around when the blackness moves in. Wait it out. Monsoons, sketchy characters, erratic film schedules, brutal authorities. Get as high as you can and wait it out.

The reason Marty gets picked up is serious. She is indeed a runaway with outstanding warrants for stupid stuff like moving violations, failures to appear and the occasional shoplifting. She's a real pro at not getting away with stuff. Most importantly though, the one thing she did get away with was several pounds of mushrooms from an uncle she was living with in West Texas somewhere. Like, duffel bags full.

He doesn't report any of this to the cops, but you're always in worse trouble with drug dealers than you'd ever be with the law. He threatens us all with violence when he finds our camp, then leaves. Luckily none of us know anything.

"Classic Marty," we all say, even though no one knows her, but we all know the type, you see them coming always, all bold and brash and in their own opinion always underpaid; a type we all should be able to write off and dump by the side of the road like we do with all the others who don't cut it. It hits me like a rock in the stomach. Adam's abusing not just his wife and kid but the whole family, all of us. Marty's using him to get what she wants, but he can't see it because he's got the open relationship going. Does he not see how pissed Eve is? Are we all being used like this?

While we're in town, I see Dawn talking to two strange guys on the street corner. The connection seems close, as one strokes her arm, and she laughs. Am I just like them? Is there a constant parade of easily manipulated young men in and out of her life? The cops write us up for peddling without a license, since Adam, distracted by Marty, neglected to buy the license we usually always run with. After a quick afternoon shuffle through the Farmington court system yet again, Adam pleads but cannot get her free, and we're ushered out the back door into a rainy night. Adam lingers inside with the authorities, and we all have a moment to talk amongst ourselves before he comes out.

"Time to leave," Lightning says, tossing his smoke into the rain. "We've burned too many bridges and the appeal of this shit is gone." He's right. Curb painting relies more than anything on the ability to remain anonymous, the "they were here and now they're gone" mystery that kept communities happy and us well-paid. We've been arrested, accused of aiding and concealing runaways, blown our covers, and we've all been picked up by the cops for the second time in less than four months. All bad moves, and the heat against us won't die now.

Our problem is we've started to believe we could actually remain in one place, become members of a community that really would just like us to disappear. We don't belong, and we've got to move on.

The next morning, we all pile in the van and drive through the dumping rain to breakfast at the local truck stop on the outskirts of town, a safe outpost when the weather turns. Safe from the storm, we order and turn to the events of the week. Eve lays it all on the table.

"What's going to happen with Marty?" She says.

Adam bristles at being put on the spot, but it's unavoidable at this point.

"Well, we can't let her stay in jail. I'm going to bail her out."

Gilles asks what we all want to know.

"What's the story with her, anyway?"

We get the duffel bag full of mushrooms story, and Adam reveals that her uncle is also her pimp. *Jesus.* Eden asks what a pimp is, Eve tells her it's a shitty, shitty boss, which seems to satisfy her. None of us are surprised, and Adam swears he's never seen anything, but I can see the wheels spin in everyone's heads: is there a giant stash of mushrooms somewhere back at camp? If I find it, can I steal it and get the fuck out of here? I don't know how clear it is to anyone else, but it feels everyone has entered split agenda movements. It's palpable and depressing. Our food is delivered. I have to ask the family.

"How many of you are committed to finishing this film? There's two weeks of shooting left."

There's hesitation, then Lightning raises his hand. Then Eden. Eventually, everyone raises their hand—except Adam. His response is typical.

"I love everything about it," he slurps up his pancakes, "fantastic work so far. You are all doing amazing work."

We get some much-needed repairs on the bus (about four hundred dollars, which, I'm guessing, based on our rate of returns lately and our spending, is about all we have in reserve at this point, even though Adam assured us there was much more), and he continues to dodge questions as we pack up our camp site, readying ourselves for whatever comes next.

Years later, I will be able to identify talk like this before it even happens. Reading people is tricky, back then I was just learning to trust my instincts. I know now that statements like Adam's bullshit noncommittal words, especially in the production of any project funded independently by one person. It can only mean one thing: *I'm about to ruin everything.*

"We're going to make some changes," Adam blurts out. If I was smart, I would have kidnapped Dawn and Ed and absconded with the monster and tapes in tow that night; take the first bus out of town, raised a giant middle finger to changes. That Amarok head, all the blood packs we'd painstakingly made by hand. My God, those blood packs! It was so fantastic to develop our own methods for something so secret. Even when we scrounged a phone number in Hollywood to ask a prop house where and how to get this information, they literally told us "figure it out, that's what you do." The character lists, the shot logs and the shooting script, all of it. Hundreds of pages, literally.

I make a vow to myself, tucked into my sleeping bag in the dirt with Ed that night as everyone else snores away in the bus: this film is going to get finished. Dawn and Ed are my real team, to the finish, but are they ready to run at the first sign of capture and/or destruction? I have plans to bolt at any moment.

In my dream that night, I am the monster. The deep, excruciating agony of being trapped in a body I don't understand, alone in a dark forest with no one to trust or confide in, a fear in my heart about what to do, where to run to. The plight of all monsters: to be painfully, fundamentally misunderstood.

Everyone stays. Adam bails out Marty, we stick it out the sake of our brothers and sisters, for a film that was mostly done, after months of prep and weeks of shooting, dedicating everything we had in us to this story, and in horror we listened to Adam's new pitch.

"We're going to make a haunted spaceship movie." He smiles and cracks his neck, as if he's said something brilliant. Arms crossed over his chest; he awaits our answer.

I light a cigarette, pass it to Ed. Everyone avoids looking directly at Adam and instead look to Dawn or myself. Adam sees this is genuinely irritated, the power struggle he feared has come at last.

Dawn and I try to communicate via eyes, but Adam is onto all of us.

"If anyone knows where the mushrooms are that Marty was hiding, turn it over. She's gone, and things around here are going to change. This movie will get finished. This is real now."

My head hurts; I'm feeling the crush of being an artist on someone else's terms, a real brain splitter. I have a hard time hiding my emotions, so I'm conjuring my best *yeah, no problem, whatever* face and attempting to keep my anger and hatred hidden. The wheels in our collective heads are spinning in all directions. The last demolition derby has officially begun. I put my psychic helmet on and prepare myself for the worst, hoping to give whatever's left of this film my best. The night turns into a day I would rather forget.

*The following pages brought to you from the glorious picnic
tables at quaking aspen campground, August (2?, 6? 13?) 1990*

INT. CITY HALL - DAY

A crowd mills about as the council take their seats, standing
room only in the hall, tension is thick.

> MAYOR
> (banging gavel)
> Order, order.

The crowd quiets down.

> MAYOR (CONT'D)
> We'll be getting right to the
> matter at hand tonight--

Angry, clean cut Mormon HENRY, 40, wastes no time in stirring
the crowd up.

> HENRY
> Should have been on this two weeks
> ago!

The crowd rises in volume, a couple 'yeahs! and 'Goddam
rights'.

> MAYOR
> Look, we've brought in agents that
> are specialists in the field, and--

> HENRY
> Specialists in what? Satanism? Cuz
> that's what this is, witchcraft!

The crowd obviously agrees by the rise is tone and anger from
the room. Another city council member, BILL, a military
looking blue collar guy, points at Henry.

> BILL
> Knock it off with the Satan shit,
> Henry. We got a case of wild,
> possibly rabid animal attacks and
> you're gonna let these fellas
> speak.

Henry finds a seat. FBI Pete stands and clicks a switch to
slightly darken the room and holds up the clicker for the
slide projector.

                    PETE
          We're aware of you concerns and are
          working to resolve this quickly.

He clicks on the first slide, an image of cattle mutilation.
The crowd groans.

                    PETE (CONT'D)
          We reached out to local ranchers
          here in your community, a couple
          have night cameras to protect their
          herds. We hoped we might find
          something that might help us find
          the culprit.

Another slide, this one of a what appears to be a massive
badger, facing away from the camera. Crowd murmurs of 'what's
that?' And 'what the hell?'.

                    PETE (CONT'D)
          We did.

Another slide, a frontal view, fangs bared like some
monstrous, vicious badger.

                    MAYOR
          What is that, a badger?

Pete shakes his head and looks out to the crowd.

                    PETE
          That, as strange as it may seem, is
          a wolverine.

Confused murmurs from the assembled.

                    PETE (CONT'D)
          Latin name Gulo Gulo, which means ← *True!*
          glutton. Twice.

                    HENRY
          No way. There's no way that's an--

                    PETE
          An animal that hasn't been seen in
          this part of the country in over a
          seventy-five years? We thought so
          too.

Ken joins him to answer the confusion.

                    KEN
          We sent the images to a fish and
          wildlife manager up in Montana, who
          confirmed the ID.

People are only more confused. They wanted a monster!

                    HENRY
          Alright, but so what?

                    KEN
          This is an animal that scares off a
          grizzly bear in the wild, a thing
          so vicious it'll attack and try to
          kill anything in its path. It's why
          they were hunted to near extinction
          almost a century ago.

                    PETE
          We believe this is the animal
          responsible for the deaths here in
          your community.

A tiny woman, KIM, 60, stands and speaks.

                    KIM
          But it's so small!

Murmurs of support in her claim.

                    KEN
          An adult wolverine is only about a
          third the size of an adult male
          bear, but it's paws and claws are
          larger. It's a freak of nature.

                    HENRY
          Kill the beast!

Two teenage girls in tie dye t-shirts, MILLY and MOLLY, both
18, stand and address the crowd.

                    MILLY
          No way! They *just said* it's an
          endangered species!

                    MOLLY
          Save the wolverines! Save Mother
          Earth!

                    HENRY
          It's a demon! We must kill it
          before it kills us! Kill the
          monster!

Bill lowers his head in disgust.

                    BILL
          Jesus, save me from your
          followers...

Chants of 'slay the beast!' and 'kill, kill' echo through the
chambers as the girls are shoved aside and the ravenous horde
moves into the streets. The tone has gone from horror movie
to Mel Brooks parody of a horror movie.

EXT. CITY HALL - MOMENTS LATER

Across the street, always watching, is Ellie, with her trusty
megaphone. A boy her age rides by on a bicycle, who she stops
and promptly shoves to the ground, stealing his bike.

                    BOY
          Hey!

He protests and tries to stop her, but she takes pedals away.
All of this goes unnoticed by the mob, flooding into the
street, torches and scythes now readily apparent, like
Frankenstein's hateful neighbors, a parody of the torch scene
from that movie set in suburban America.

24

INTO OCTOBER WE SHOOT, torches lit, the coup of filming illegally in a little abandoned city office on the edge of town with multiple extras to form a mob should feel like a victory, but it doesn't. No ideas come from the rest of the crew so I improv some real torches for the mob, rags and kerosene. Everyone seems to have lost their steam.

Then, overnight, Fred and Morgan take flight. Poof. They escape with the paid-off van and some dried food. I lose my temper. Fred and Morgan were awesome not only as friends but as family. I'm done keeping it together, then do what I've done my whole life when I can't control a situation or feel powerless. I find a wooden ax handle and decide to destroy something inanimate.

This film is teetering, almost finished now, and I don't know if it's victory or defeat, realizing I've got no control over the outcome, not just of this film but my entire life. It's impossible to clear my head and if others are leaving, why shouldn't I? I destroy, swinging again and again, smashing the rear of the bus, crushing metal and smashing taillights, red plastic shards exploding everywhere until finally, the handle splinters into pieces, my hands a bloody mess. I scream, sweating like crazy, realizing everyone is now looking at me like a crazy person.

"What the fuck are you all looking at?" I say, tossing the destroyed handle and storming into the trees. Best to walk away after a show like that.

Evening comes in and as the sky darkens, I find a pottery shard and use it to lacerate my arm. The more blood I spill, the better I feel. Pain is a great way to escape one's own thoughts. As the heavens open, so does my arm, blood and water flow in a mixture of frustration and madness. Finished with my little tantrum, I stumble back to camp, honest about the fact that I'm an idiot and now going to need stitches. I wrap my arm in my T-shirt to try and hide the stupidity. As if that's possible.

Twenty degrees that night is followed by a sunrise that hands us eighty degrees before noon. Sniffles and coughs, complaints and criticisms. Wet sleeping bags and damp, dark attitudes. My once cheery demeanor has turned to an aggressive, hyperbaric mental state that I can't get out of.

The bus roof has started to leak, and repairs are not forthcoming. Adam and Eve are constantly arguing, whether about Marty, or the film, or the business, who knows. The puppets and paper mâché heads start to melt from the wildly variating moisture and heat. Fish & Game Wardens approach, telling us camping is indeed free on BLM land, but making a film is not. We're handed a booklet of rules about insurance and licensing procedures and fees for filming on federal land. The gig is up. When they leave, we finish the day's shoot, a quick couple dialogue scenes with Lighting recording audio like a pro, as always. We all pile into the bus as the sun sets and have a tense but ultimately productive production meeting.

As the bus ceiling drips and little pools gather across the floorboards, we all call each other out. Eden levels the playing field.

"Daddy, you're angry all the time. Why?" He looks genuinely hurt for the first time in months.

"I guess the stress of living out here drives us all a little crazy, honey." She climbs in his lap. We've all been swept up in it and it's time to clear the air. Ed calls me out, his hand on my shoulder.

"You gotta stop being such a baby. Lashing out like that, it's stupid."

He's right, of course, and we do a round robin in recompense. Dawn answers for her indifference, and Adam for trying to call all the shots. Everyone participates, both in making claims and responding to them. We all want this film, this life, to succeed, and stating it in brazen terms and conditions leaves us feeling better, if exhausted. We all hug and plot our sleeping areas around the puddles collecting on the floor, laughing by the end at our misfortune. Eve makes sure to get the last comment of the meeting as the candles burn bright.

"Yeah, housekeeping? What about this ceiling, Mr. I Can Fix Anything? I swear to God..."

"I'll fix the holes tomorrow," Adam says, as we drift off to sleep singing "Fixing a Hole." In the morning we'll break camp and soldier on.

With a somewhat renewed sense of purpose and hastily patched rooftops, we hit it, again. Paint some curbs in Springerville, stop off at Strawberry Hot Springs, where Charlie Chaplin and Mary Pickford used to visit, taking a quick soak to recoup our minds.

Given time, wounds heal and while we're still on edge with Adam's new dictatorial sense of control, what's the worst that can happen? He was always the one in charge, it's just that now, even people on this ride much longer than me voice concern over his self-aggrandizement in recent days and weeks. I'm driving the bus one morning when I get utterly confused by road signs. I thought we were close to Tucson, turns out we weren't even in Arizona. We're in New Mexico? Colorado? Borders are fake, false identifiers of a stable land, and truth be told I have no idea where I truly stand from day to day.

To get back to where we were, financially, we weren't above straight up begging as well. When you're hit, don't stay down. We all take turns asking strangers for spare change at rest stops. The take can be good, and Heather and Dawn can wrangle thirty or forty bucks in an hour. We hit (old hippies) Sedona to paint and pump up our cash reserves a little more. The towns are small and tough along the way. The neighborhoods are tiny, and we already hit Prescott once last spring, just on the other side of town. The people are friendly but the returns are abysmal, another forty-dollar day for ten people. All our hired actors are now gone as we've shot most of their scenes, and the bus feels, for the first time in a long time, empty. In all it takes almost two weeks to get back to the suburbs of Flagstaff, the promised land in terms of smooth, new curbs. Ugh. Flagstaff is a dead man. No more good curbs to paint, anywhere. Eve's map has run out, at least until the spring of '91, so we turn east again.

We make our way back to Houston, a city with more cops but no limits to suburban sprawl. I take the wheel again, and with Lightning and Ed following in the Honda as we deadhead east, the warm night wind in my face as the moon rises in the east, I reflect on the last ten months.

I flash back to my abandoned attempts at formal education and think about Dawn the instructor. Dawn the slayer. Dawn the braggart, the down and dirty angel with a head full of light. She is a comet that slammed into my planet and started in motion a series of events that will eventually repopulate my world with thoughts and ideas, things I will later brazenly steal and call my own.

Halfway through Oklahoma, we take a right. We cruise through the Chickasaw nation and head south into Texas at midnight, my mind uninterrupted and turning everything over as the bus hums along, a card game going on the floor behind me, everyone now laughing and gambling, again.

We come into this world, the world of life on the road and wild abandon and ever wandering, with our thumbs out and boots falling apart, music filling our heads and bones, and we take what the road gives us. Some of us are running away, some are running toward. We get what she gives, sometimes freely but most often by force. We make a world out of whatever the rest of society has left behind, tossed and forgotten. We make music and magic in the dumpsters, forests, and abandoned campgrounds of America's lost worlds, hidden places out behind the strip malls, where streetlights rarely work, and address numbers don't exist anymore, if ever they did. And when we take a pride and ownership in these things we've created; we fall into that same trap that makes the world go 'round: I, me, mine.

Is this film worth fighting for? Is it something we grab and say, 'this is ours and we're not giving it up?'

Absolutely. We laugh at the laws of this land. Our film will tell our story to the world: we existed. A splashy world premiere in Hollywood? A film festival somewhere in Europe? At the very least, a screening somewhere in Northern New Mexico. Maybe a projection of our desires, dreams, and nightmares onto the side of a building somewhere? An audience full of lawn chairs and brown bag bottles being shared freely among an audience of roustabouts? The love in this thing is pure.

Eve directs me into a campground a few miles east of Houston at four in the morning, everyone now asleep. I pull into a slot, shut it off, grab a pillow, put my feet up and fall asleep right there in the driver's seat. We have five pages to shoot left. The end feels so close.

25

THE NEXT MORNING it's clear something's wrong as I roll out of the bus. Dawn is yelling at Taz while Lightning and Heather try to calm her down. Gilles is talking separately to Taz and Caveman in hushed tones. Ed is on top of the bus with a giant art pad and pencils, sketching it all. What the hell is going on? I notice the Honda is gone. Then, I hear Dawn say it. That term I'd heard way back in January, "next phase," has finally been revealed.

I'd caught the phrase a couple times since but lost concern the deeper into the family I got. Maybe I assumed I'd be included? Nope. Adam, Eve and Eden are gone, disappeared in the Honda. Money? Gone. Film? Gone. Cameras and scripts? Gone. Maps? Gone. All gone. Taz and Caveman seem to know something, and in Dawn's mind, Taz is the one to break.

"What's 'next phase'? Where are they?" she asks, pushing him against a tree. We try and get her to back off, but she isn't having it.

"This punk knows what their plan is, I know it."

"Do you?" I ask, wanting to deescalate and get some answers. Taz looks to Caveman.

"Don't look at him, look at me." Dawn shoves him harder, making him squirm.

"I...she's..." Taz struggles with conflicting loyalties.

"Eve? She's what?" It seems likely she's going to punch him.

Caveman finally blurts it out, attempting to save Taz from violence.

"Adam went to talk to a guy about a sailboat to buy and sail to the Bahamas. Or something." His eyes dart around nervously, he knows he just betrayed Adam.

And there it is. All along there was an alternate agenda, a secret kept hidden from the team of friends gathered around this hustle. Turns out we weren't the only ones with a boot bank account.

"Where? When?" She throws Taz to the dirt, standing over him. Gilles tries to pull her back, but she shoves him off too.

"Fuck off, Gilles. We need to go. Now. Unless, of course, you have any money at all?" She glances at Gilles, wondering if he too banks with the boot brothers. He shakes his head.

"Right. We're fucked." She kicks dirt at Taz and steps away.

"Eves at a hotel in town, getting a shower and taking the day off. They'll be back. That's all I know. Honest," he says as he sits up, spitting dirt from his mouth.

"What hotel?" She strides to Caveman, who doesn't need to be asked twice.

"I don't know. We don't. She'll be back tomorrow, maybe the day after."

As Dawn fumes, Lightning quickly starts packing up our gear.

"Everybody load up."

"What are you doing?" Gilles asks, as Lightning continues folding blankets. Lightning smiles his toothy, devil grin.

"I know where they are. Same hotel from last year, I guarantee it. I got a nose."

Everyone tries to hesitate, but Lightning and Dawn are dual igniters now. Dawn barks orders.

"You heard the man, load up! Let's move!" Everyone moves, throwing things into the bus. We're out in less than a minute, bouncing down the forest service road towards space city from our campsite on the outskirts.

An hour later, we're there. Sure enough, Lightning knew where they were and by doing the old sleuth number, he spots Eve smoking cigarettes on the balcony of the Ramada Motor Inn on the east side of Houston, right off the 10 freeway. We converge after hiding the bus on a side street.

"He'll be back," Eve says as we all barge into the room. "He'll answer all your questions. Just don't worry, don't worry." We're worried. Especially when we find that all the footage and the camera equipment is gone.

We spread out to search the hotel's garbage cans and dumpsters, just to make sure Adam didn't dump everything and leave it somewhere we could easily find it. No such luck. Fuck. I imagine him somewhere across town, waiting for a pawn shop to open, ready to sell the gear. Gilles does a quick sweep of nearby streets for the Honda as well. Nothing.

Dawn loses it and attacks Eve, smashing up the room in the process. Heather and I try and stop them, but she's out before the cops arrive. A fistfight in a tiny hotel room with several people trying to break it up damages pretty much everything in it. In an inspired move, Eve tosses the

TV at her, then smashes her head into a mirror, shattering it. Even I got a black eye. We all fall back, hiding with Eden in the bathroom, door closed.

Bleeding, Dawn launches herself out of the room and into the streets of Houston, kicking several cars, setting off alarms and sending everyone out to their balconies to observe our unfolding drama. No one cares when you tear up a campground and smash a bunch of stuff. When you pull a rock star on a legitimate motel in Houston, cops are pissed.

We have a quick council in the parking lot after the police leave and decide to stick around. Unless he's abandoning his wife and daughter here, let Adam return, bring back the hostage tapes and hopefully give us at least some satisfaction in the knowledge that we were always more than what we've become, not opposing forces but a temporarily divided clan, eager for a forum to talk through our grievances. Fat chance.

For me, it's to get the film, and hopefully, some closure. We sleep in the bus across the street from the hotel, monitoring the situation, waiting for the captain to return. As I try to drift off, my thoughts about burning friends and escaping into the night betray me. I can see myself, and I hate it. I've become the monster.

Next day, we make the choice: paint every curb we can. It's the last of the fliers, last of the glass beads, last of the paint. Use it up, wear it out. Houston is full of new neighborhoods, always building and growing. We avoid the permit and go for broke. The vibe that we're all in it just for the money now is strong, and while that was always true thanks to our nomadic existence, this feels different. This is the month it's going to happen; secretly we'll each pocket as much cash as we can and when we get the opportunity, we're gonna rob each other and hit the road, a clean getaway.

My plan is simple: continue to lie to myself and pretend it's all okay, my actions are necessitated by the exploitations of others. That night I dream that I'm rising, up into in the air, face down, over a massive forest. The apocalypse felt nearby, but here in these woods I was safe. I couldn't stop rising in the air. All around me trees, nothing but endless trees.

We find an old neighborhood that has, for some reason, never had its curbs painted and maintain our strategies and work in teams. We are all trying to forget the pain of this makeshift dream as we place our fliers on every screen door of all the little houses. Hopefully Dawn will return, it's Wednesday but in my mind her deadline is Friday—Halloween. My hope is that we catch Adam, steal the film, abscond with enough cash to Greyhound it back to San Jose, encamp to a little place in the hills above the San Francisco Bay where some friends are living, start editing.

We've got a monster movie, and since we've shot enough footage to relate the story to an audience, I figure if we can swipe the tapes back from Adam, there's a great film there. Sadly, that seems to be a bigger and bigger if. There's a story in those tapes, the horror of not facing our responsibilities as Americans, and what happens when you ignore the words of the elders.

My desire to find this film is causing me to consider foul play. How fucked up is that? Not that I'd do it, it's just the mind of the young artist, right? Writers think about murder all the time, right? Everyone thinks about killing to get what they feel is rightly theirs, yeah? My comrade in cinema, my partner in crime is a leader in absentia now, even while we work the streets of Texas.

The question for the others isn't "When's Adam returning?", it's "When's Dawn coming back?"

We flier a thousand houses in one day. One thousand screen doors receive our clarion call to the community, hard to ignore and simple in delivery, as always. We've broken records and tomorrow we'll paint like our lives depend on it. We go morning to night, with Taco Bell pit stops and bathroom breaks in local parks and community centers. It's weird; looking back I think we all knew what lie in the days ahead, and whether Adam returned with our film or not, it was a do-or-die week.

We grab food at the 7-Eleven on the way back, power down nachos with that horrible cheese that is so delicious, microwaved burgers and burritos, forties of beer, and bags of chips. Then straight back to the Ramada to check if Adam has returned. We find Eve and Eden still alone, and out of money. None of us want to believe Adam could do this, but here we are. Eve is hurt, but ever resilient. She's been making calls. A friend in Phoenix, his folks in West Texas. No luck.

"Let us know if you hear anything." The line goes dead, she sighs and hangs up. Now fully out of money, they move back into the bus with us across the street, packed back in like those first days in January, all sleeping together, close and warm.

For tonight, we're secure in the knowledge that tomorrow will be the curb painting day to end all curb painting days. We buy a cheap twelve pack, smoke the last little bit of dirt weed before we hit the hay. Because we're in the city, no one can sleep outside and the cramped conditions force Ed to sleep in the driver's seat, while Lightning throws his sleeping bag up on the roof, a lookout in case Adam shows up in the dead of night. We are all splayed out like a sleepover, the first time in a while we've slept this close in that dear old school bus, laughing and chatting before sleep takes us. Our bicycles are loaded down, baskets full of stencils, shakers full of glass beads and the last blast of the spray paint. We're ready. I fade out listening to the echo of Houston's streets throughout the bus, a cavernous interior, a cascading, repeating drone of tires on asphalt, the car lights passing by like a dying projector, the sound of voices in the distance, a world so removed, so close.

Tomorrow is Friday. Halloween. Dawn doesn't return.

26

WE'RE UP with the sun and the streets are calling our names. We're right about the neighborhoods, and it's better than we imagined. The teams start early, which usually for us is nine. No breakfast buggers, we don't want to catch Dad on his way out the door, and we want to catch Mom before she heads off to shop or work herself. But today, fuck it. We're on bikes and painting by eight. And returns are, while not the twenty percent we hoped for, still really good. We catch people around the house, it's seeming to be a holiday for many, and people want to grab one last summer day, even though here it's truly fall—an Indian summer for Texas. It's going to warm up today, you can feel it, even at a frosty seven thirty in the morning. Blue skies appear through the quickly dissipating mist. The Halloween decorations remind us that we're almost done for the season, too. Leaves glorify the morning, all red and yellow, falling in clumps at the curbs and having to be swept away by slept-in boots and jeans. Today there's a sense among all that this is our end of the year. We wear sweatshirts and caps. Store-bought cornucopias stuffed with plastic squash and pumpkins grin from every porch, harbingers of the cold streak that awaits us all.

I work with Ed all morning, and the amount of people that have paid already is ridiculous—Ed's pockets are literally bulging with cash. We laugh as he has to pawn some off on me to keep it from looking too comical when he provides change. Just between the two of us, we pull in over four hundred dollars before lunch. We decide we'll return half to Eve, the rest will disappear into private pockets only to reappear in safer, more hospitable climates. On Halloween, no one takes notes.

We paint through the day. Our fingers are covered in black and white spray paint and glitter glass. The teams meet for lunch at a Taco Bell; we're all killing it. We're going to clear a thousand today, easy. Lightning jokes that we should just head out, start a fresh team, put some jack o' lanterns on our heads and blend into the crowds, drift away, buy another van, start anew. We did all the work, after all.

Then Ed reminds those of us that don't know, the last time someone tried something like that, Adam followed them to Colorado to get revenge and claim his territory. Nine-hundred miles for a miserly three hundred bucks. I had heard the story of a long pursuit, à la Butch Cassidy and the Sundance Kid, but I didn't know over what. No one seems surprised, and we all agree, grudgingly, to hold the line, to finish Texas and get a new group together after we've made sure the girls are alright and provided for.

No one mentions the film. I don't bring it up, in the hope that someone, anyone, would dare to share how important it is to them. It isn't. It was Dawn and I all along. Lunch is over. Sensing my sadness, as we walk out, Ed puts his hand on my shoulder.

"Your movie is the best, man. I'm glad to be in the company of a real writer, a true filmmaker to the core." We hug, and I am close to tears, filled with love for this cat named Ed.

"Thanks. That means a lot, buddy."

"Good. Because I just made that up to make you feel better. Now let's get the fuck back to work."

We laugh and laugh. This is the way our days went, truth infused with humor and scalding sarcasm to temper the heat of living a life so crazy and loose, always so near to disaster.

We climb back onto our bikes and prepare to finish the day in a dazzle, all the ghosts and goblins that scurry about drive our energy up and light the flames on the funeral pyre of our merry little band. Come what may, the witches are out tonight. Light 'em up.

Ed and I grab a six-pack of beer and power down three each in the alley before our last run.

Kids run around screaming and laughing, getting a jump start on the festivities. We're asked several times what our costumes are, but 'curb painter' doesn't seem a satisfactory answer. While everyone paid, this one homeowner really makes our day. It's the old maxim, if you knock on enough doors, the wizard will eventually answer.

This guy was pushing seven feet tall, with that Burt Reynolds 'fake macho' look. Big moustache, helmet hair, coke bottle glasses. Nice enough, but definitely goofy looking. We had just painted his curb; all we had to do was collect our eight bucks and hit the road. We had several more streets to paint and wanted to finish as quickly as possible. He was initially confused, and a little bit upset. We had to explain it a couple times. Either this guy is high, or we're drunker than we think.

"There was a flier in your living room window," says Ed.

"I didn't put it there," he gruffly responds.

"Well, we painted the address as requested." Ed points to the flier in the front window.

"I didn't ask you to do that," to which Ed follows up with the flat, emotionless,

"Well, the cost is eight dollars." Ugh. Hoping he won't call the cops, we walk him in his pressed slacks and tucked in western shirt to the curb to see that it's there, facing out in all its reflective glory, so firemen, delivery people and the like can better find his home. He looks at it, looks back at the house, sees the flier in the kitchen window and says, "What the heck is that?"

"That's the flier, man!"

Without a word, he walks back inside and we see him pull it out of the window. He returns, staring at it, says, "Oh – you guys are artists. Right. Okay. My wife told me."

"Sure, yeah, that's it, artists" we say. His switch finally flipped on, he turns and says, "I got your money. Sorry. I was confused, and it's Halloween, so, you know. Come on in." We follow him inside, more annoyed than anything and wanting to get the hell out of here so we can wrap up the day. We wait in the living room as he goes to get the eight bucks.

As we wait, we see one entire wall is lined with hundreds of 8mm and 16mm films, all organized and filed on custom wood shelving, a thousand titles in a kaleidoscope of color and fonts. Like if you walked into a museum in, say, Kansas, and you're confident there's not going to be much going on but the first thing you see is a bunch of shotgun art by William Burroughs? And how it kicks you back a step? Do you know how it feels when that light goes on, when the magic is proven to be true and right in front of you? It's incredible. A treasure trove of film history, his own little cinematic library hiding out in suburban Texas. Amassing a small collection of my own as a kid, I'm impressed. I step closer, wanting a look at some of the titles.

"I wonder if he's got *Abbott and Costello Meet Frankenstein?*"

The slim cases are hard to read, so I lean in closer. I see *The Blow Job Kid, White Sisters in Peril, Honky Go Lucky, Ilsa, She Wolf of the SS*, and a bunch of German and Danish titles. A lot have swastikas and Gothic symbolism scattered throughout the spine art. It's a bunch of porn, and a lot of it seems close to, if not literally, rape/fascist/white power films. These are hard core short films. Decades of them. This shit is obscure and dangerous. I don't get weirded out easy, but this is making the hairs on my arm stand up. At least we're still just a couple feet from the front door.

He returns, sees us checking out his collection and gets excited. Now I have to do that thing where I act like I'm not freaked out. Yes, I *am* interested.

"I also collect old films."

"What are the chances? Well, we have something in common." He hands Ed the eight bucks, thankfully, since my palms are sweating. "Here's a ten, keep the change."

Ed has to walk forward to him, standing just outside the living room, in a little back hallway, to grab it. It's like he's dangling it, trying to trick him to come forward, and it sure doesn't help that he's got a psychotic grin on his face. I'm about half a second from bolting when Ed grabs the bill and the tension breaks. Years later, I'll be starkly reminded of this moment in the scene from *Silence of the Lambs* where Buffalo Bill goes to hands Clarice the business card, waiting for her to come forward. A "draw them in" kind of thing.

We turn to walk out when he says, "Well, you have to see my monster mask collection downstairs then!"

Ah shit, monster masks? Gotta be quick, the day is dying.

Ed looks to me, smiles and shrugs.

"Alright, just a quick look, I guess."

He and I share the look that says *if we have to, we'll kill to get out of that basement.* I'm not positive what he's thinking, but we seem to be on the same page. Hopefully.

We descend into southern soil, a narrow drop off into the inner chamber. Basements may or may not be common in Texas, but this one was dimly lit, with a single bulb over the staircase barely tall enough for us to walk down, let alone a now painfully hunched over giant of a man, casting a sliver of light into the darkness beyond. Talk about a horror movie. This guy barely fits down here, and it would be comical if I wasn't so fearful that things could go south in a second, ending our short, pathetic lives.

Recalling that Ed carries a nice little hunting knife in his waistband, I'm a little less frightened. Reading my mind, however, he whispers "I forgot my knife on the bus" as we reach the bottom of the stairs. On come the lights.

Across the span of my life, I've collected thousands of records, comics, books and assorted ephemera of my favorite films. My uncle opened one of the first underground comic shops in America, my dad owned auto dismantling yards full to bursting of beautiful, abandoned magic, I knew thrift from trash and shit from shine. but this is something else entirely.

An original head mold from *Creature From the Black Lagoon*? Check. 50s-era werewolf masks? Check. Original Verne Langdon Zombie Mask? Check. And many more. There are probably close to fifty masks, molds, assorted lobby cards and posters displayed throughout the small space, all lit up with red-bulbed wall sconces and little special spotlights on the posters. Unable to contain our enthusiasm, we tell him about Amarok, confessing our production woes and trials and tribulations, everything that's going wrong for us right now, and how we're funding this film by curb painting and most importantly how close we are to finishing the film. He seems genuinely impressed and takes on a different tone.

"Well, that sounds like a lot of work in some pretty desperate conditions. But the story sounds great! I commend you for launching into such an endeavor, living out of your vans and all." It's like we've crossed a barrier and now the tension is gone, he's the father figure now, and so he lets us peruse the masks for a few more minutes, peppering us with helpful if odd anecdotes about finishing projects and "hanging in there, just like that old cat," he says, pointing to the director's name on a *Castle of Blood* poster. Suddenly, he whisks us back upstairs.

"Sorry boys, almost forgot—have to finish my special Halloween dinner." We have to know: who is this guy? This is a wild mix of both amazing and sketchy film history. We enter the kitchen as he pulls a massive knife and cleaver from their drawers to begin dissecting the mass of meat, origins unknown, on his gigantic cutting block. I'm distracted as the blade slices through the meat like soft butter; it looks like he's preparing asada. With his intentions now focused on the meal at hand, we grind him from across the kitchen island with a few quick questions before we head back to our curbs.

"So, what's *your* origin story?"

"I was born in Pasadena and grew up in Burbank. By fifteen I was working in the film industry, doing whatever it took to keep some money rolling in. Lots of odd jobs on those lots in those days." He slices away as he reminisces.

Thank God I'm working with Ed today. I always respect his patience and ability to see, not just right now but almost always in this crazy year, what we need as opposed to what we want. He helps me stay focused and inspired, even up against a ticking clock that pulls the sun towards the horizon and reminds us that while we're excited to hear this guy's Genesis tale, he better make it quick.

He made his living Hollywood, starting in the 50s. He was a runner and a coffee boy, a page riding his bike from set to set delivering updated pages, scripts and various contracts to assorted directors, actors, etc. He moved on to working on B movies and monster movies, ending his small-time career as a property master on the little-known 1980 film *Alligator*. He scored most of his collection from dumpsters in studio lots and location shoots across Los Angeles. He's the original Hollywood dumpster diver! He'd been doing it with a couple friends from the early 60s onward. This guy blows our minds, and suddenly—whoosh—we're out the door, dodging witches and ghosts as they dart past us, looking for candy.

We wave from the street, he seems as pleased as we are to have had this unlikeliest of meetings happen, maybe more. Magic is real. Monsters are real, just not in the way most of us imagine them. His parting words, the advice he gave will stay with me forever, sage advice that I scribbled in a journal will survive many long, strange years later.

"Don't stop, don't ever stop," he tells us. "When circumstances beyond your control force the abrupt end of something you're building? You don't finish your film? Fuck it. Make another one. Next."

27

ED AND I are focused on three things: finish this day, get that money and escape into the west, with or without Dawn. I am so despondent about the film; I can't let it get into my head that it's gone. I try focusing on everything else, going full nihilist on it all, ready to cash out and head into my next adventure which I was confident was just around the corner. And then, as if the universe knows only how to respond to personal desires with chaos and frustration, Dawn returns.

She and Eve have apparently reconciled over motel room coffee and donuts. Who knows what was said. Whatever it was, they seem to have squashed their differences and seem to have a common sense of completion. Eve sends her to us in a last-ditch attempt to fuse back together any last chance we might have for the family.

As all teams meet at the agreed upon Taco Bell for what will be our last supper, Dawn is there and is concerned about one thing: The film. Everyone is happy to see her but wary now, even me. Her inclination towards violence has shattered her standing with the family, and she knows it. I cut through the shit and ask her before we even enter the restaurant.

"Did you find the film? Or Adam?"

"Nothing. Fucker vanished."

A despondent look on her face reveals it as true.

After a round of hesitant hugs, we all gather at a table in the back that Ed commandeers as our last supper setting. I have no plans on burning anyone specifically. It's more of a general "I'm taking my portion and heading west" cowboy on the lam scenario. Dawn tells us that she and Eve are united again, but to all present, that's not enough. The damage has been done. She's the squeaky wheel, but no grease will be forthcoming. What hurts most is what I slowly come to realize as I eat my burritos and nachos. The film is more important than our relationship. Like me, she seems disinterested in anything other than the film.

This film, like our lives, holds within its imagery a testament to all our attempts, a snapshot of our efforts and successes, failures and defeats, casting nightmares and puppetry genius. There is a college degree's worth of study, testing and satisfaction in that footage, far beyond anything I was goofing around with in San Jose. She wants it back. Amarok is both awesome and ridiculously inept, a sassy, freaky art project to the last. I feel drained, exhausted to the point of abandonment. I don't want to die in here.

I keep telling myself it's nothing personal to make me feel better. It's Halloween, crossover day between life and death. I tell everyone that it's going to work out, privately plotting my own escape and I have to lean into the staying together theme, so no one doubts me. Gilles speaks first.

"You got any bright ideas on how to move forward?"

"I do," I reply.

"With the bus, we can make good money here for the next several weeks, with or without Adam. If, at that time, he hasn't returned, we can head back west for the rest of the fall."

I'm so full of shit it's embarrassing, but everyone buys it. Almost everyone. Ed and I have secretly split our own skim, a little more than we said we would. If the other teams even did near our numbers, it's clear that today, October 31st, 1990, in Houston, Texas was gangbusters epic returns. My guess? Two thousand dollars, maybe more. Everyone looks very happy as we dump the remaining cash and curb books with filled orders across a table that looks like it's been cleaned with grease. The vibe I'm getting is we're not the only ones who pocketed some twenties for an unknown future. When there's so much to go around, banking with the boot brothers feels almost clean. We bag it all up and head back to the bus to grab Eve and Eden and do trick or treating right. As we all exit the restaurant, Dawn takes me aside.

"You still want that film too, right?"

"Of course," I say, lingering with her so we can speak privately.

She tries to lure me. "I want that film, but more importantly—I want you."

She's so full of shit. I have trouble swallowing the last of my burrito, but no problem looking deep into her eyes and seeing the real her, the truth of her, wanting to hold on to a life that simply cannot continue to exist. She hates when I stare at her and say nothing. I'm double crossing her, lying and pretending I care about things I don't. I'm ashamed that I'm getting so good at lying in pursuit of answers.

"Really? You're ready? No goodbyes? It's that easy for you?"

"It is for you, isn't it?" she's says, trying to avoid my eyes. I say nothing.

"Let's go get candy!" yells Heather, already costumed up in what will become the default costume of every woman in the 90s: the sexy witch.

We break out our Amarok props and become a groovy, post-punk posse of monsters and mutants, leading our little girl around the neighborhoods. Eden is dressed as, and in fact has always been, our Angel. We've finished off another twelve pack and look like the extras from a Gwar tour. While some neighborhood parents have donned the occasional witch hat or face paint, most are without costumes and interact with us at arm's length. In other words, we're having a blast. We polish off a bottle of bourbon as well, shrieking laughter deep into the evening. We return the girls to the bus parked in a cul-de-sac around the corner from the hotel, another perfect place to spend the evening. Lightning checks in with the hotel office: no Adam. We feel bad, it's looking like he may have left the girls. Gilles, however, says that he and Heather will stay with them, no matter what.

With Eve and Eden tucked in, we walk to a nearby bar which is still going strong at midnight. Everyone else comes along, a last rally and party, toasts to things not yet known and celebrating things we had done and how much it all means to us. The band is loud, and we're all yelling over each other about how the stories should go.

Lightning is pouring shots in everyone's mouths, a girl he smoked weed with in the alley has snuck in a bottle and we brazenly drink them with her, sharing with monsters and wizards, escaped convicts and nurses, zombies and hoboes, and then holy smoke bombs, the band launches into "Shake a Tail Feather" by Ray Charles and everyone loses their minds, dancing like maniacs. Out of nowhere, a 3-piece horn section dressed as ninjas appears onstage with the band and drives everyone over the edge. We devolve into mad joy. The place is packed and wild, sweaty and primal, a throbbing thing from beyond the grave, a primordial sway and as the band drives to the chorus, even the bartender loses herself in

ecstatic head banging. All participants, no observers. The applause and laughter afterwards ring in my head to this day. Watching a three-way make out between King Tut, a zombie, and a nurse is something you'll never forget, I don't care how drunk you are.

Most of the gang eventually departs, but Dawn and I dance with the madding crowd until the last song has been played. She tells me that we should get the hell out of here after we've settled the girls and re-established the team with or without Adam, head back to the West Coast and start anew. It looks so good on paper, it's true—love's a difficult equation. I may be drunk but I'm not a fool. I know her claims of wanting to stick together is a clutching at straws scenario to save her own ass, not mine, but in an attempt to keep the night alive, I lie and I acquiesce. Like her, I've learned to tell people the stories that they want to hear. I overheard Ed earlier in the evening talking in the bar to a girl about heading back down south with her, to New Orleans. Something about a cotton candy factory. The band finishes the night with a Dylan classic, "Quinn the Eskimo."

I'm so drunk I can't climb into the bus. I hit the ground, chaos coming to rest, feeling safer here on the sidewalk. I want to be left alone. In my heart, I know the film is gone and it hurts like nothing has ever hurt before. It's just…gone. It's over, all over.

It's three in the morning, forty degrees out, and the streets have quieted. Dawn enters the bus, returning to bring me my sleeping bag and a pillow and then, instead of re-entering the bus, she walks away. I lay on my side, drunk, head on a little dirty pillow propped on the curb, watching her walk into the night. I want to get up and follow her, but from under the bus my point of view is beautiful, fully cinematic.

This would be a great angle for a shot of a woman leaving a man, I think.

I'm crushed. We won't make it; I can feel it in my heart. As she walks away, silhouette lit up by faded halogen streetlights, long shadows burn in my brain of what this year is doing, has done to me. I've come undone. Trying to focus as I lie spinning on the sidewalk and staring across at her from under the bus, I notice something else. A dark, dirty object stuck in the undercarriage of the bus. It looks like an old trash bag, probably caught by the wind as we drove. I roll off the curb and into the gutter to inspect, reach up into the chassis.

Trick or treat. Runaway Marty, as foolish as she was, found a magic hiding spot for her stolen stash. An old Adidas gym bag stuffed with mushrooms, looking like trash that got stuck up in the rear axles of the bus, held in with bailing wire. Her satchel of psychedelics, two, possibly three pounds, wrapped within another, dirtier looking bag. I have seconds to decide, to try and focus—I'm still seeing double. Everything starts to move incredibly fast.

I grab the bag, trying to be quiet as I yank it free and drunkenly sprint after Dawn to show her the magic gym bag, eager to win her over one more time.

"Oh, I was coming right back." she said. "I was just going for a stroll."

She tells me she's planning on sticking it out a little longer. How true that is, I'll never know. Better to go down as a team, even if the team won't last. I reveal the contents of the bag, wanting to use the mushrooms to hold onto her as long as possible. I suppose if I just stole them and disappeared alone, I'd feel like more of a thief. Better to bring a couple along with me in case the scene gets nasty. If I meditate too long on the lost film, I'll want to murder someone.

So here we are. Adam's taken our movie, lost to the wind. We can't find it, or him. Should we hunt him down, attempt to get it back? The wheels spin in our drunken heads and where previously there seemed to be little hope, we now have an option. We wake Ed and drag him out of the bus and have a quick powwow curbside.

"Yeah, I'm in," he says. "Let's break for it."

We enter the bus as quietly as possible and collect all our notebooks, a couple cassette tapes of audio, one videotape of monster shots and cutaways, illustrations and shot logs, anything remotely related to our documents that prove we exist. Dawn writes her parents' address on the wall of the bus in sharpie, I do the same. Lightning snores away. This is it. Immediatism. A dead of night departure.

This bus has been our home. It's hard when you feel so much good will and love for a physical place, even a transitory one, a place that rolls through time and space and has the capacity to keep your hopes high, your heart pure, and your dreams clear. We made a fucking movie, for God's sake.

We screamed "cut!" a thousand times, directed hapless actors and wrote horrible lines, tried to synch sound devices in rainstorms and heat waves, made a mess of campsites with pools of fake blood that surely frightened the hell out of whoever showed up there next; we truly made a mess of it all. We wasted thousands of dollars, spent in the name of freedom and happiness and none of it would have been possible without this old bus. It was all a glorious, colossal waste of time, ill-advised. And yet? I cannot advise it more passionately. High now on adrenaline and escape energy, we move in silence, but then I turn and see Eve, sitting in the driver's seat, rolling a cigarette.

"What'd ya think, I was gonna shoot ya?"

She steps outside, lighting her smoke. We walk down those magic stairs for the last time. I am thinking of details, trying to remember it all as I know I will never be here again. As I clip my backpack around my waist, the faint click resonates throughout the bus and makes me look around once more. Five steps down, that giant door handle armature that controlled who came and went, the mirrors that reflected what we do and how we see.

At that moment I knew it. Should we make this escape and not get caught by Adam, we would never see any of this, of them, ever again. When you give up your seat on a ride like this, it has the tendency to disappear into the world. Step, step, step, step, step. We walk down the gangplank and seal our fates and forever cast ourselves as outsiders, cast and crew no more.

We're on the street, and that's when the sadness in Eve's eyes hits me like a sack of rocks. We're abandoning the woman who needs us most, I think. We stand with her and smoke one last cigarette. She has no knowledge of the mushrooms, but she realizes the better part of her team is leaving, on Halloween, her favorite holiday as well. We try and make excuses as to why, trying to make ourselves feel less bad, but she cuts us off.

"You guys were fun. That movie thing was fun. And no, I don't know where the film, or even Adam, is. But we've been gone a long time. Don't feel bad for me or Eden. We'll get a new crew together, even if he doesn't come back. In America, there's always new curbs. The road goes ever on, over rock and under tree and all that shit."

Eve quoting Tolkien right there in Houston at three in the morning on an abandoned sidewalk as her silent partners plan to break for it makes me tear up. She hugs me.

"Don't lament. I'm thankful you all came along when you did..." I stare at her beautiful face, perfectly framed by her strawberry blonde hair, always a bit scruffy, so endlessly cute and adorable. She is really a doll, one cool woman I will truly miss for the rest of my life.

Dawn slams her with a hug that lasts over a minute. Both women are in tears.

"I love you, you crazy bitch," says Dawn, through tears and kisses as Eve wipes tears from her eyes.

"I love you, too. Can I have my sunglasses back now?" They both laugh, and as Ed and Eve hug, Dawn digs through her pack, coming up with what I thought were her sunglasses, the fade cool aviators. She puts them on Eve, who turns to me and scratches my head like a dog.

"Good boy!" Everyone laughs, all silently thanking our lucky stars that brought us all together anyway. Eve is so committed to life on the road and freedom I can't help but cry as I hug her again.

"Tell him I want that film. I'll pay for it. My contact info is on the wall by the emergency door."

"Yeah, he's probably already traded it for speed anyway," she says, mocking me, ridiculing the thing she knows I miss most. I laugh, weepy and jeered at by friends and family, a testament to my life here. Hugs go around once more, then it's time to leave. I'll always carry this with me, this way of looking at the world, this way of being so alive at the end of a cosmic century. I came into this by accident and now, I must leave.

In ten years, the millennium will come, and across its teetering edge will ride an ancient school bus loaded with freaks and curb painters, dropouts and weirdos, mangy musicians, dirty dogs and kids who say no way to a new world order. At once hidden and fully exposed, the bus will set sail into a brave new world. And in my heart, then as now, I'm always there.

Slinging our backpacks over our shoulders, we finally turn and walk away. I begin to sing the song Eve knows so well, the rounds we all learned, formed around fires of long, long ago.

"Road goes ever, ever on, over rock and under tree, by caves where never sun has shone, by streams that never find the sea…"

Eve the ever knowing, singer of a thousand songs, all loving, jeers and jokes by the dozen, a mother and a sister, sometimes complacent but never unkind or mean- unless you deserved it. We stride into the night, streetlights casting long shadows, disappearing into the future. Ed plays along on his flute, sealing the moment in amber, forged in campfire and cast in reflective curb numbers.

The three of us foot it across Houston, a horribly long walk for drunk people with loaded backpacks out of a dark, tired civilization. The bus station is miles away and there is a nine o'clock out of town heading west. We're going to be on it. The sun rises over Texas as we stumble towards our destiny. Goodbye to the garden.

DAY 244

(things to remember: listen to primus and mudhoney, see david
vostell film *the being from earth*)

Ext. Rundown trailer- morning

Ellie rides up to the trailer, sitting out alone by itself on
the outskirts of town. She dumps the bike and steps inside.

INT. TRAILER- SAME

The Shaman sits on a battered couch watching game two of the
world series, ignoring Ellie's presence. She plops on the
couch next to him.

                    ELLIE
          You know, the development has been
          abandoned. It's not just-

He raises a hand to quiet her. The pitcher is about to throw.

                    ANNOUNCER (ON THE TV)
          Stewart looks to first, gets a nod
          back.

Ellie is mad, but the Shaman remains glued to the pitch.

                    ANNOUNCER (CONT'D)
          And here comes the pitch to
          Hatcher...

The Shaman sits up as the crack is heard.

                    ANNOUNCER (CONT'D)
          It's a hit! It's way, way back...

Ellie stands up and lets the play finish (an out), then turns
off the television. The Shaman leans back, looking at the
ceiling, then out the window avoiding her gaze.

                    ELLIE
          Fine, don't look at me. But please -
          it's over. Please. Let him go. He's
          done here.

Using his cane, he stands and looks down at Ellie, making her
look small.

                    SHAMAN
          It is already done.

Ellie looks concerned.

                    ELLIE
          Then why is he still killing?

                    SHAMAN
          Perhaps this is a question you
          should ask of it.

She looks flustered but stays focused.

                    ELLIE
          But where'd it go?

The Shaman looks out the window and points.

                    SHAMAN
          There.

They both see the Amarok, in full daylight, sagging to the
ground, tired and falling apart. Blood everywhere, it is
dying.

                    SHAMAN (CONT'D)
          It needs your help.

                    ELLIE
          With what?

                    SHAMAN
          Help to the other side.

Ellie goes out the door.

EXT. TRAILER- MOMENTS LATER

String arrangement music starts here, some somber, slowly
climbing fugue with a piano joining in, a rise from distant
to dominant across this last scene. Like Mozart's requiem in
D minor or something.

She approaches as it gives off a sound like a dying animal,
lying on it's side. She walks closer and closer, closing the
gap between life and death.

They are now face to face, her look one of kindness, of
sadness and sorrow. The Amarok seems to see her, or at least
sense her, but it is mostly dead. It's massive, disgusting
eye blinks.

CLOSE SHOT WITH JUST FACES IN FRAME - SIDE TO SIDE.

Ellie raises her hand to its face, a move that causes the
Amarok to respond to the gesture with a whine, like a
wounded, dying dog.

INT. MISSILE SILO -DAY

Looking up into a blue sky, framed by the metal grate, steel
slats like the sides of a reel of film, sprocket holes.

We watch the dead carcass being shoved over the edge and into
the abyss by Ellie. She struggles with its bulky, inhuman
shape, but gets it over, the edge of no return.

In slow motion it tumbles, antlers, head, torso a shredded
cage of bone and blood, a collapsing pile of dark magic, into
the dark, no longer needed in the world of the living.

FROM BELOW, the camera zooms slowly, slowly up, out of the
hole, rising to a close up on Ellie's face, rimmed by the
blue sky, as she struggles to comprehend the meaning of it
all. A monster that was desperately needed and had a job to
do, yet in the end destined to die, discarded and alone.

The sadness on her face a combination of incomprehension and
disgust, tragedy but most of all - release.

_____

_____

28

THE BLINK OF AN EYE transports us as far west as we can go without falling into the Pacific. The ride from Los Angeles to Santa Barbara is even shorter. After crossing half a continent and zigzagging across half a dozen states for almost a year, this is a blip on the radar.

Ed bails out in Arizona to head to Mexico to catch up with some sheepherders and score some wool for hats he wants to make. He writes down the address of a buddy in Santa Barbara who he says can put Dawn and me up at his mansion, then he's gone.

Suddenly, and for the first time, it's just the two of us, left struggling to find what may or may not be. Working through it together, with agendas and projects, gives a couple purpose and tends to give love meaning. I am thinking of a new story to write as we approach the gates of the address Ed gave us.

Upon arrival, we discover the house was sold, we are told to leave, and that was that. We walk north of Santa Barbara and make our way down to a tiny hidden beach, accessible only at low tide, perfect for a private encampment for two.

We set up our tent and stash our gear inside, spending our days laying in the late fall sun, dumpster diving the local supermarkets and thrift stores and make extensive notes about what we did right and what we did wrong with our film. We slide into the back rows of some lectures on film at UCSB before winter break, splitting up and fitting in, looking more like theater and dance majors, but when you're young enough no one ever asks for your credentials.

I get the bulk of a three-week presentation on silent film, from the birth of cinema to the end of the silent era, forever forging my love for that magic era. Dawn takes in a lecture series titled Anatomy of an Industry.

We spend Thanksgiving rolling naked in the tent, making wild turkeys blush and coyotes howl in concert with us as we dive again and again into our aggressive brand of rise and fall sex magic. Our small AM radio blares out the first of the season's Christmas tunes as we lie in post-coital bliss, eating dumpster-dived pizza. We listen to Christmas carols as we swim in the Pacific.

By candlelight over the next couple weeks, we write a story together, an idea for a revenge thriller set in the world of silent cinema and taking us right up into the modern age: *I Await the Devil's Coming.*

But it's all too much. We're honest with each other and both openly admit—we're not ready for this, for each other. What are we going to do, normalize the current, cut back on the madness and get married, have kids? We're young and both want so much out of life that we dare to speak the truth, to say 'next' and move on. Being alone can mean everything.

I'm lying there in the tent thinking all this as Dawn swims in the freezing Pacific. When she returns, as she sits drying herself off, I say what's been on my mind all morning.

"I think we'd be better off going our separate ways." I look at her face.

She averts her eyes but nods her head, her face breaking into a sadness previously unseen. Did I guess wrong? Was she ready for the long haul with me? For a moment I'm terrified. I feel like I'm able to see something hidden in her, the sad monster, the heartbroken monster, the understanding monster.

"Yeah. Me too." She crawls over and lays her head on my chest. I try and say something deep. It feels stupid as it comes out of my mouth.

"We came pretty close though, didn't we?"

She laughs through sniffles, responding with the kindest thing anyone's ever said to me.

"You are one weird cat, baby. Don't ever change."

We both cry a little, because we both know it: we're too attached and letting our relationship change us in ways recognizable as lame and ridiculous. Her reasons are her own: on a phone call home to Canada, she's told that there is a position open in her friend's circus that has been doing really well, and a European tour next spring that they want her on. I feel the love of her, the loss of her, the lament of what could have been and the joy of being free and open to new worlds yet again all at once. It's all too much, it's all never enough. And now, it's all over.

"We have to have a make out session to remember each other by," she says.

"Really? The bookstore was enough for me," I say.

"You're a liar."

"That is not a lie. I will tell that story for the rest of my life."

She laughs, that throaty snort-laugh that I will miss like crazy. "Do you remember the title of that book you were reading to me?"

"*The Principles of Psychology* by William James," I tell her. "What was yours?"

She cocks her head, as if thinking of it for the first time. "I have no idea."

Great. I'll have to make it up.

She laughs, throws off her towel and we end the relationship like all good people of this earth should; in the embrace of something too pure, too powerful to hold onto and knowing that even if you tried, in the end it would burn you beyond recognition and make you into that thing you most despise: A normal couple, doing normal things with normal people in normal places. A fate worse than death.

I go for a swim alone later that afternoon, paddling out far enough to look back and enjoy the sight of our tent with a small fire smoking beside it, a magical little picture, pushed up against the sandstone walls that protect the rest of the world from the sea. It's a perfect snapshot, and as I tread silently in the flow of the ocean, looking back, I catch a glimpse out of the corner of my eye of a coyote up on the ridge. I turn my head to see it more clearly, but it disappears into the quickly gathering mist that covers the central coast so often this time of year. Freezing now, I paddle back in, watching the ridge, trying to catch a last look.

Grabbing my towel, I dry off and enter the tent. The first thing I notice is my skateboard is missing. I frantically search, whipping through my stuff, realizing now there's only one of everything: a sleeping bag, a backpack, some food. Her stuff is gone. I whip out of the tent, eager to catch her, but it's too late. I close my eyes and let out a sigh, and taking a deep breath I go back in, thinking *she wouldn't dare take my skateboard, would she?*

Flipping over my sleeping bag, I see something I missed before, a little postcard lying where my board was, one from the last dive we did together. An Indiana postcard, from the old times, unused and so out of place in a New Mexico dumpster, a beautiful snapshot of fall in the east. *Autumn in*

Indiana, it says.

I'm pissed, but I have to laugh. I can't fucking believe it. She took my prized board, my Mark Gonzales Street model with the speed freak wheels and in return leaves me a note. I know it's true before I even flip the card over, revealing her perfect little cursive handwriting, her script so small I have to hold it closer to read it. One line.

"Thanks for the ride, babe…"

Every house is a madhouse. Every home an asylum and every wall in America is, in its way, the split personality of institutions that have spent centuries being trained how to divide us and teach us to obey, to remain within. We must break out, we must escape and run for the hills, either literally or figuratively. The forests are calling, the cities of strangers are alive and await us, and we must all go into the wild, wherever we may find it, if only for a time. Magic and danger await those of us with enough naïve excitement, wrapped in the desires of youth and the madness of drink and mind-altering drugs, bold and brave enough to walk away, if only for a moment.

I often had the feeling of being an escapee, lucky enough to have broken free, outside the walls of complacency and bills, timeclocks and collar shirts—tucked in please—and lame, jokey conversations that drag one through most of existence. The rumors you've heard are all true: there's more.

My inadvertent kidnapping had dumped me into it, lucked out in finding something pure and wild. A deep, aimless river flowing through the heart of America, an aggregate of ideas and time, blended into that beautiful cocktail called youth. The wild of the Southwest gave me time to ponder America's relationship with herself: those places between and within the realms of curbs, the gutters between normality and madness.

Most of us will stay put and allow ourselves to be numbered in a thousand meaningless ways, whether it's our curbs, our timecards, our cars or our camp sites, shrugging it off and saying, "what can you do?"

This place is full on crazy, and to truly enjoy it you've got to get out into it and participate in the best part, the borderlands of the American experience. Beautiful small towns and unknown cities, wide open plains. Abandoned nuclear missile silos. Junk yards and back alleyways, from the campgrounds to downtowns. Streetlights and starlight.

In the end, Dawn takes the one video with footage we still have and disappears.

"I'll copy this and mail it to your parents' address," she promises.

It never arrives. I search high and low for both her and the tape, years later, but it seems that, like all great lost lovers, she simply disappeared into the world. I never see nor hear from Dawn ever again.

29

SLEEP FOR DAYS. Can't write, can't get out. I find myself missing the tide patterns and get stuck several times in the inlet, trying to climb the steep rock surface with my pack, almost killing myself, then shrugging and going back. Depression sets in like another wanderer setting camp in my heart, promising nothing.

Was that it, I wonder? Am I doomed, destined to be alone and always wondering "what if?" Is that all I got from all this year, no film left, not even a photo, but instead, a sack full of mushrooms?

It all feels pathetic as I set up my tent again and lay out my sleeping bag and roll. I eat nothing but cans of sardines and crackers, doing push-ups all day and meditating, writing crappy poetry.

A couple days pass, and I start to come out the other side. I'm cleaning out mentally, taking account, building little fires with the last of my kindling and trying to straighten my thoughts into some cohesive way that will allow me to return to the land of the living.

Everything that went right on our film, everything that went wrong, all accounted for in longhand lists regarding what I would've or could've done. Singing sea shanties to myself, about monsters and nightmares, alone and tired, looking forward at last. I've been so far gone that the place I'm from, the world I'm planning to return to isn't even clear anymore. It's only been a year, but it feels like a lifetime. I can never be the same or truly revel the way I once did in my old ways.

The me that left is gone for good, and returning is a being I barely know, ready to take its place in my own mythology. Will anyone know the difference? It doesn't matter; I do. My transformation now begun, I intend to continue to evolve and transform into a new thing, constantly. I may be a monster, but I am an understanding monster. Not a dark thing, brought forth for personal revenge or some other such maleficence. I am born again, of the road, a wanderer and a creator, a child of the west.

I know that somewhere several hours north of this beach, my old friends are skating ramps, laughing, jamming on cheap punk instruments, living a life uninterrupted and clear. I long to return. The rains come. I stay in the tent, day after day. A week passes, then almost two. It's too much. I've overthought it all and now it's Christmas Eve. Honoring the magic of the season, I eat a handful of mushrooms, scale the wall and walk the four miles into town, a holiday pilgrimage into California's original theme park.

Santa Barbara is lit up, Christmas lights tangle through the trees lining the busy streets, clichés spilling from the mouth of every passerby. For someone who has lost a lover and now lives in a tent, I find the platitudes of window shoppers and people on their way to Christmas parties refreshing.

It's a pleasure just to be in one place after running across the country non-stop for the last year and to just sit in a coffee shop, conversing with strangers, to read the newspapers and get caught up on reality.

I call my mother, who is overjoyed at my voice, safe, coming through the line on Christmas Eve. She tells me about my sisters and my father, how everyone wishes I was there, which makes me feel shitty so I just go ahead and tell her I'm in California and will see her soon and hang up. The night suddenly feels like a landing. I've closed in on my native land and the vibrations tell me I'm about to go ashore. I've worn my last great dumpster score, a white leather trench coat, and with my long dirty hair and aviator glasses I catch myself in the window of a hardware store.

I laugh, realizing I look like some wild seventies' version of one of the three wise men. Tonight, I am the Magi.

I stay late into the night. Many shops are open, and Christmas Eve always drops a sort of magic on places in my memories. I drift into a house party pumping with the new sound all the kids are going on about— techno. I stay late, drink a few cocktails and when at last I wander back to my camp, the sun is beginning to rise.

I've learned what generations of American adventurers, wanderers and dropouts have discovered before me—life's true nature is only found by avoiding the terrorism of tourism and climbing on board an old, battered bus and sailing directly into the heart of the sun.

You must be broke. You must dumpster dive. You must spend time with the people who so desperately love this place, who were born and raised here and will live and die here, despite the differences of all its vast peoples.

There is no place like it, rising red cliffs in the east dropping off to blue skies way out into left field, a stripper named Amber Waves, licking the hot borders of her plains, swaying to the beat of a hundred million years come to rest, in a place called 'the west.'

The aggregate I painted thousands of times became the coarse material through which my own life began to take form. My lifelong wanderlust set in motion by my year there, I returned richer than I could have imagined. I walk away unattached, with no girlfriend, one hundred and forty bucks, a duffel bag full of mushrooms, wearing a white leather jacket. In other words, I win.

The Greyhound pulls into San Francisco exactly one year to the day I was spirited away and forced to live my life, to find within what I wanted to see without. December 31st, 1990. I'm back in the city, and I await Jim's rambling Chrysler Cordoba, the same battered beast that transported me to my appointment with the future twelve long months ago. A lifetime ago.

"No Dead show tonight, man," he promises in a pay phone call the night before. "There's something else, something better." I raise my eyebrows. I just want to sleep, but I humor him.

"Sounds cool."

"Yeah, it's called a Rave. See you tomorrow."

In true dramatic fashion, Jim speeds into the Greyhound parking lot on Mission just so he can screech to a halt, scattering kids and adults alike. He doesn't give a damn as people curse him, a chain-smoking white boy from San Jose, dirty long hair and tie-dye shirt and pants, cranking gangster rap at top volume with a huge smile on his face. He exits the car to give me a hug, then a bow and a "may I grab your bags, sir?" as he hurls them violently into the back seat of the idling Cordoba, smiling. Another born comedian. As we enter the car and head up Fell Street, he alerts me to his dilemma.

"Been tryin' all week to score. From Santa Cruz to the City, man, everything in between, I'm telling you. Weed, mushrooms, acid, I can't find shit. Everyone's either dry or in jail. You like speed?"

I shake my head. He lets out a heavy sigh, sad at the idea he's let me down. He is my drug dealer, after all, so it's normal for him to feel like he hasn't done his job when he comes up empty.

I reach into the back seat and pull the satchel out of my bag and zip it open, revealing the pounds of mushrooms. His reaction is priceless. His eyes bulge as he stares, becoming so distracted he sideswipes a parked car on Laguna, crushing its mirror and doing minor paint damage to both vehicles in the process. We howl as he roars away, running a red light, both of us watching the rear-view mirrors for cops.

He lights another cigarette, eyes on the road, and then, with perfect timing, "No one saw a fuckin' thing." We explode into laughter.

At the next light, Jane's Addiction's "Been Caught Stealing" blares from the car next to us. Jim looks again into the bag. He nods his head in approval and pats me on the shoulder. The light turns green, we speed up Fell Street, into another New Year. Nothing left to do but smile, smile, smile.

CUT TO BLACK – ROLL CREDITS

Epilogue

There were other roads to take. New outlooks to embrace, more wayfaring strangers to join up with and rattle our marching drums into a new millennium. I became many things in my first year on the road: a poet, a dumpster diver, a lover, a leader, a curb painter and a thief. I was a fire starter and a rabble rouser, a song writer, and a guide. But most of all—I became a filmmaker.

In 2023, curb painting for the most part feels like a dead scene now. For many of us who saw the beginnings, so too is punk, dumpster diving, and true underground scenes, those last bastions of true hidden worlds, stopped short by a generation of 'lifestyle brand' corporations, litigation-happy sleazeballs who tried to seal our fates, locking dumpsters so no one could file a lawsuit if they fell in, removing diving boards from motel swimming pools so people can't sue, stripping down the American Dream, one case at a time. But I hope I've made one thing clear: it's still there.

The profession of curb painter is not extinct in today's economic landscape. The time when you could raise a family on this madness, running back and forth across the continent, endlessly weaving into weird American slipstreams and subverting normalized suburban lifestyles, often in the course of a single afternoon may be mostly lost, but it's out there. I recently returned to the Southwest to find plenty of neighborhoods with unpainted curbs. It still exists. It's not easy. All you must do is ask yourself: am I ready to skip out, to test the waters? Find passage on a ship that will take you there. Maybe you already own that ship.

This lifestyle is not for the delicate—everything was pretty much insane all around us, all the time, much to our enjoyment. Fragile, easily intimidated folks might want to hang back and just read the book, watch the movie, listen to the podcast. It's a wild, magical life out there, and it promises everything you may desire, or fear.

It's a new century. You can still be a drop out and make a go of it. You can still be a roadside prophet and mechanic, entertaining the wayward breakdowns with jokes and a smart set of tools that helps get others back in the game. You can be Huck Finn or a Bodhisattva, you can be the hero of your own drama, or you can be me. It's right to embrace multiple roles, types, and voices in your own quest into the great unknown of yourself and a thousand more in this life and dive straight into that great world out there, just outside the door that can prevent your escape only if you let it. Check and see. I told you: it's unlocked. Open that shit up and walk the fuck out.

You can visit amazing places and do amazing things with amazing people and come out the other end. You will not remain unscathed, nor should you. You don't have to be young—*just go*. Go now. What I love about America is that so much of it is unfinished, so undiscovered and unknown. We relied on new developments of suburban sprawl to fuel our own fires, but that got us closer to the truth of the thing. By knocking on doors and letting ourselves be exposed for the kind of people we truly were, those homeowners I was once so glib about in turn exposed themselves and shared their lives with us, deepening my understanding of real monsters, of villians and secret paths to a life less painful.

This story comes from a place too wild, something I've gotten used to in the telling of so many of my tales. The fantabulism is too much for some. From wrecking yards and punk shows to Cathedrals and mining villages, remote forests and high-rise office work at the end of a too stupid century, it often seems made up. Who the hell gets in a knife fight with a goth girl in front of the fun house at a county fair in rural New Mexico? We do. With a few notable exceptions, the trip was real. And no trip is a success for me unless I've taken every opportunity to throw myself fully into it. There is so much in America left to discover, so many heroes and monsters to meet and forge alliances with. I hope to do it again, and I hope you get the chance to do the same.

Note: That nuclear missile silo is the site of what is known today as the Titan missile museum. Our crew of madcap travelers were literally the first inside that insane monument to man's capacity to destroy the world since it had been intentionally flooded and filled with water in 1982. There's a neat website about it now with a schematic of the place we entered, more clearly defining the layout. Check it out.

This book is dedicated to my one partner and true love, Elizabeth. You have never wavered in your support of the mad ways in which I create.

Ridiculous and Ill-Advised was edited, many times over, by the amazing Cooper Lee Bombadier at Indigo. His unwavering destruction of my first drafts were instrumental in creating an actual, readable story. I cannot thank you enough.

Sections of this book were first published in Gravel magazine.

Edward Wesley Hale, my co-pilot on so many roads unknown, thank you for introducing me to Adam and Eve and the road less traveled. We put our trust in the magic of the two-lane, a wiser move I've never known. From the years of our youth up to today, you are truly my brother in arms.

Thank you to Steven Pinker for use of his lines from his book The Language Instinct.

Thanks to Vince Font at Glass Spider Publishing for all his support and helping get this monster off the ground and into the world.

Film reference list:

All the films mentioned, either slipped into the story secretly or in conversation, are required viewing. See how many you caught.

Faraway, So Close
The Thing
Investigation of a Citizen
Halloween
A Woman Under the Influence
Ivan the Terrible
Battleship Potemkin
Wild Strawberries
La Strada
The Passenger
Two-Lane Blacktop
Piranha
Barton Fink
Faust
C.H.U.D.
Texas Chainsaw Massacre
The Hills Have Eyes
The Birds
Raiders of the Lost Ark
Who's Talking Over There?
Kings of the Road
All That Heaven Allows
Prophecy
Nomads
The Being from Earth

www.ingramcontent.com/pod-product-compliance
Lightning Source LLC
Chambersburg PA
CBHW031508120626
46545CB00005B/1789